INTRODUCTION

These colorful talismans, pronounced OHO-DAY-DEEOS, were originally made in North America by the Pueblo and Mexican Indians. But they are much older than this, for they appear in the tombs of ancient Egyptian rulers, wound of fibers from the Nile river banks. In fact, an eye appears on the pyramid of the U. S. one dollar bill. On a recent trip to Northern Europe, the author found 200 year old ojos in the museums of Scandinavia, modern day ojos in Poland, ojo jewelry in the marketplaces of Finland. No one is sure when the first ojo was woven of simple sticks plucked from a bush or shrub, and wound with river rushes or vines, but even before Christianity man has used the shape of the cross to invoke protection.

Part of a North American Eskimo collection now in a museum has an apron on display. It is a ceremonial garment worn during religious ceremonies and is made of butter-soft deerskin elaborately painted with designs familiar to most of us as part of totem pole designs. On the apron appear more than 25 eyes, all assuring protection to the wearer, and through him to the entire tribe.

God's eye talismans have been found in such places as the South Pacific. In Northern Australia, a god's eye design has been found among the aborigines. In Fiji, the god's eye symbol is used on their war weapons (See FIJI FAN).

The early Indians, whose ancestors are believed to have come from Egypt, were perhaps only renewing an ancient belief when they sought good health, good crops, good fortune from an ojo made to be displayed on the walls of their cave dwellings. Today the modern Indians still perpetuate the custom of asking for protection from a being more powerful than their chiefs.

Although the making of ojos has become an art form, refined to fit the sophisticated homes of today, the simple beauty of their execution has persisted. They may be made of nylon and metallic threads rather than growing vines, but their meaning is the same — May the Eye of God be on you, and bring peace, plenty and happiness to your household.

There is no more sincere way to say "I wish you well" than to make a gift of an ojo; and no better way to pay homage to ancient beliefs than to make an ojo for your own home.

TERMINOLOGY

Attaching yarn: Unless otherwise directed, yarn is always glued on back of ojo arm with cut end toward left and ball of yarn toward right. It is then brought to front by flipping ojo frame to the left.

Eye or top wrap: This means a simple wrap covering each stick in rotation counterclockwise, working from the front of the ojo at all times. When used as the start of the ojo, it forms the eye at the cross of the sticks. Used as the ojo progresses, it is known as the top wrap. (see **Diagram A**)

Double eye wrap: Occasionally an ojo is designed to be hung as a mobile, or placed so it can be viewed from both sides, as in a room divider. Then it is necessary to wrap both sides at the same time. This is done by passing over 2 sticks, returning to starting point, then passing over the next stick in rotation as in the regular eye wrap. This is repeated until the eye is the desired size. (see **Diagram B**)

Oblong eye: When sticks are glued at any angle other than 90°, a square eye will not result. An oblong eye is wrapped by crossing between two sticks to cover center then wrapping as directed. With a two stick ojo, the eye will be wrapped on each arm. With a three (or more) stick ojo, directions will indicate how to wrap. Resulting eye, in any case, will be oblong in shape.

Back wrap: The method for back wrapping is the same as top wrapping only the back wrap is done on the back side of the ojo forming a recessed framing when viewed from the front side.

Changing from top (or back) wrap to back (or top) wrap: There is no need to glue off when changing from one wrap to another. Simply give the yarn an extra half twirl around the stick to bring it up on the opposite side and start wrapping from other side of ojo. Be sure to complete a round before changing.

Wing wrap: The decorative arrow effect of this wrap adds much to the ojo design. It is done by wrapping opposing arms (e. g. 1 and 3, 2 and 4, 5 and 7, etc.) with a top wrap while passing under the other arms. In doing the wing wrap, the long strands must lie smoothly on the back of the ojo to produce an even "mitering" of the yarn on the wings. When trimming a wing wrap, the outline wraps must be applied to each set of wing wraps before moving on to the new arms for the next wing wrap. The wing wrap represents the Indian arrows, used in ojos as a protection from evil. (see **Diagram C**)

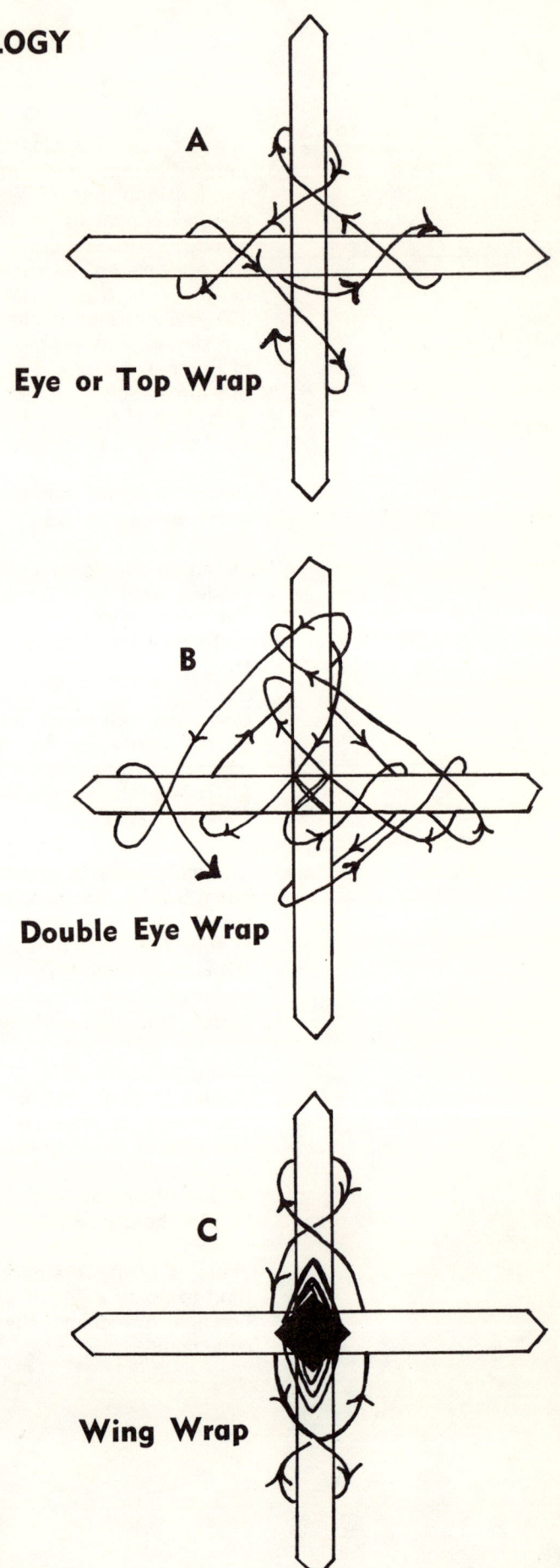

A

Eye or Top Wrap

B

Double Eye Wrap

C

Wing Wrap

THE REGIONAL CREATIVE OJO BOOK

by

Diane Thomas

Copyright © 1976 by Diane Thomas
Hunter Publishing Company
P.O. Box 9533
Phoenix, Ariz. 85068

All rights reserved.
Library of Congress
Catalog Card No. 75-44654
ISBN-0-918126-02-9

TABLE OF CONTENTS

Introduction	3
Terminology	4
Relevant Facts and Sources	7
Making Ends Neat	8
Center Trims	9
From the 50th State:	
Aloha Lei	10
Maui Wood Rose	11
Hawaiian Orchid	12
Pele's Comet	13
Kanehoe	14
From the Southwest:	
Concha	16
Christmas in Arizona	17
Navaho Brave	18
Six Flags Over Texas	20
Hopi Kachina	22
From the West Coast:	
California Catamaran	25
From the East Coast:	
Seminole	28
Sarasota Spiral	29
From the Deep South:	
Alabama Star Shower	30
Grandmother's Quilt	32
Grandmother's Fan	34
From the Pennsylvania Dutch Country:	
Hex-A-Gon	35
Barn Owl	36
Hex-A-Gram	38
Tannenbaum	39
From South of the Border:	
Fiesta Time in Juarez	40
Las Flechas de Sol	41
From Here and There:	
Party Time	42
Planter Pole	44
American Space Shuttle	46
Fiji Fan	47
Titania	48
Colors and Yarn Substitutes	50
Making a Template	51
Helpful Hints	52

ALL OJOS ARE COLOR ILLUSTRATED ON PAGES 26-27 OR ON BACK COVER

TERMINOLOGY (Cont.)

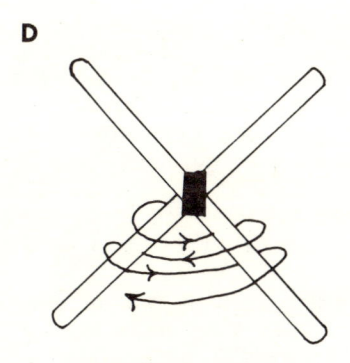

FIGURE 8 WRAP

FIGURE 8 WRAP: This wrap is worked on only 2 arms at a time. The yarn is wound in a figure 8 pattern over the top of the first arm, crossed between the first and second arm and wound from behind the second arm. (See Diagram D)

TRIPLE FIGURE 8 WRAP: This wrap is used on a 3 stick ojo. Glue yarn on arm 1, wrap over arm 1, under and around arm 2, over and around arm 3 with 2 wraps, over and around arm 2, under and around arm 1 with two wraps. Repeat for designated number of patterns. Remaining 3 arms may be wrapped in the same pattern when called for in directions.

SPIDER WRAP: A two round top wrap used to fill spaces in a 3 stick ojo, or to top-accent a 4 or 6 stick ojo by a spidery skipping of every other stick in wrapping.

STAR WRAP: This is done by top wrapping every 2nd arm in an 8 arm ojo for a desired number of rounds, always passing under the skipped arm or arms. Then attach yarn to next arm in sequence and repeat alternating wrap.

EXTEND WRAP: This is used to open spaces in the ojo for a more lacey effect. The yarn is wound smoothly around the sticks, one at a time, until the covering is the length desired. A variation of this is to connect the extend wraps. Instead of gluing off each time, the yarn is carried from the end of the extend wrap on one arm to the beginning of the next. To be effective, the extend wrap in this case must be at least 1½" down the stick before moving on to next arm.

SPACE WRAP: When doing a space wrap, as in **TREE** or **KITE** shapes, the yarn is wrapped two or more times around an arm instead of the usual once. Anytime the yarn is "bunching" on an arm, an extra wrap may be taken to help it lie flat.

CANDY TWIST: A very effective trim which can be used to outline wing wraps, define changes of color, or trim the outer edges of an ojo is obtained by tightly twisting two colors together as you do either a top or back wrap. Tension must be snug on this wrap since the two strands of yarn may tend to "roll" on previous wrap. When doing the twisted wraps, premeasure the number of rounds you intend to make, add an extra 6" for each round, and cut yarn to avoid tangling.

CHEVRON TWIST: This is a variation of the candy twist and is accomplished by doing the candy twist for one round, gluing securely, then reversing the twist by "spinning", the two yarns in the opposite direction through your fingers as you top or back wrap. A little practice will enable you to make a chevron design as the two twists lie together.

TENSION: There is no way to gauge perfect tension except to try a few rounds. Too tight tension will cause the sticks to break; too loose tension will make an unsightly ojo. Doing is the way of learning.

BASIC OJO CROSS: A basic ojo reference in this book means a simple 90° angle cross with the two sticks being notched in the center and each arm being of equal length.

SHIELD FRAME: This is any ojo frame made of 3 sticks glued together at center, whether in a 45° or 60° pattern.

HEXAGON EYE: When a shield frame of 3 sticks is wound at one time, each arm in rotation, a hexagon eye results. In this case, no skipping of sticks is done, and eye must be started by crossing in an X pattern for 2 or 3 times before wrapping each stick. This is also called a **6 POINT EYE.**

DIAMOND EYE: Working on a basic ojo of 2 sticks, take 1 turn around arms 1 and 3 and 2 turns around arms 2 and 4. When measuring, measure along the long side.

HALF-EYE: When winding a wall tree wrap, the ojo eye will only be on 3 of the 4 arms, thus a half eye will result. The measuring is the same as a regular eye — along the side.

FLOWER EYE: On an 8 arm ojo (shield frame), attach yarn on arm 8, wind over 3 arms (arm 2, counting original arm 8 as one arm), back around arm 1, over 3 arms (arm 3), back around arm 2, over 3 arms (arm 4) back around arm 3, over arm 5, back around arm 4, over arm 6, back around arm 5, over arm 7, back around arm 6, over arm 8, back around arm 7, over arm 1, back around arm 8. TO MEASURE: measure across as in top wrap. (See GRANDMOTHER'S QUILT)

ROSEBUD EYE: On a shield ojo of 8 arms, do 4 rounds working only on arms 5, 6, 7 and 8. Then wrap every arm in sequence for 4 more rounds. (The arms 5, 6, 7 and 8 are on the lower ojo. Center of ojo of arms 1, 2, 3 and 4 will remain uncovered and must be trimmed with a button, etc.

TERMINOLOGY (Cont.)

SPECTRUM WRAP: (Used on a 12 arm ojo). Color A is glued on designated arm with cut end to left when facing back of ojo. Color B is glued directly beneath as closely as possible with cut end to right. Both colors are worked at once, first the color A, then color B. This wrap is used on a 12 stick ojo. With color A, wrap over arm 1, under and around arm 5, over and around arm 9, under and around arm 2, over and around arm 6, under and around arm 10, over and around arm 3, under and around arm 7, over and around arm 11, under and around arm 4, over and around arm 8, under and around arm 12, over and around arm 1.

With color B, under and around arm 1, over and around arm 5, under and around arm 9, over and around arm 2, under and around arm 6, over and around arm 10, under and around arm 3, over and around arm 7, under and around arm 11, over and around arm 4, under and around arm 8, over and around arm 12, under and around arm 1. Be careful each time you return to arm 1 to lock colors together with a twist on the back side.

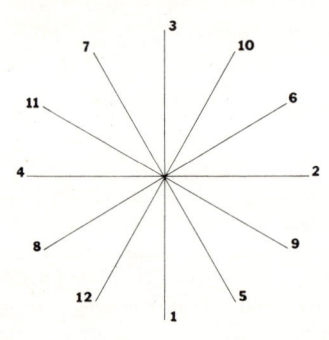

WALL TREE WRAP: A wrapping done on only 3 of the 4 arms of an ojo so wrapping is all on one side. It is done by attaching yarn on arm 2, wrapping over arm 2, over arm 3, over arm 4 with 1½ turns, back across face of ojo to arm 3, over arm 2 with 1½ turns and back across face to arm 3, etc. See diagram.

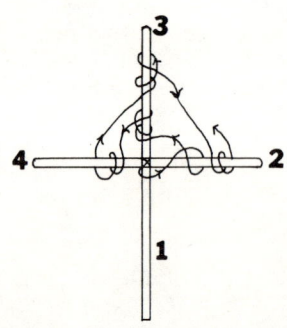

DOUBLE TREE WRAP: Glue yarn behind arm 2. Top wrap over arm 2, over arm 3, over arm 4 with 1½ turns. This brings ojo around to back side facing you. Go over arm 3 and over arm 2 with 1½ turns. Right side is now facing you. Repeat this, wrapping only arms 2 to 3 to 4, back to 3 to 2, back to 3, etc. This result will be a half-eye (since arm 1 is not wound), which is measured along the side as in a regular eye. When gluing off or on, always complete front and back wrap; e.g., 3 rounds will then be 3 strands of yarn on front side and 3 on back. End on arm 2.

TRIPLE STAR WRAP: Used on a 12, 18 or 24 arm shield ojo. Yarn is wound over one arm, skip two arms, wind over 3rd arm until returning to starting arm. Yarn is then glued on next sequential arm, wound over that arm, next two arms skipped, over next arm, to starting point. Pattern is repeated until all arms have been wound.

OBLONG STAR WRAP: This is an alternating arm wrap done on a 3-stick ojo. (See PELE'S COMET, page 13)

DOUBLE WRAP: Yarn is wound over two sequential arms twice, then over second arm. e.g. Glue on arm 1, wrap over arms 1 and 2, back around arms 1 and 2, then around arm 2; over arms 2 and 3, back around arms 2 and 3 and around arm 3, etc., winding on both sides of ojo at once.

DOUBLE COLOR WRAP: Two yarns are worked at same time in reverse windings. Attach color 1 on any designated arm in a basic 4 arm ojo with color 2 directly beneath but coming from opposite direction. With 1st color, wind over 1st arm, under and around 2nd, over and around 3rd and under and around 4th, returning to starting arm. With 2nd color, twisting threads to "lock" color 1, wind from under 1st arm, over and around 2nd, under and around 3rd, over and around 4th and return to start. Repeat number of times directed.

FAN WRAP: The fan wrap is used when the ojo frame is an incomplete circle. With top wrap, go over and around each stick in succession until the last stick is wound. Taking an extra turn to bring yarn under the second time, backwrap across to beginning. Taking an extra turn on left hand stick, return to top wrap. Continue in this pattern. (See GRANDMOTHER'S FAN, page 34)

VERTICAL DIAMOND WRAP: A vertical design is obtanied by wrapping two turns around arms 1 and 3 and one around arms 2 and 4. This will elongate the wrappings in a vertical plane.

VERTICAL DIAMOND SPACE WRAP: When a sharper vertical delinination is required, three turns are taken around arms 1 and 3, and one turn around arms 2 and 4.

HORIZONTAL DIAMOND WRAP: A horizontal design is obtained by wrapping two turns around arms 2 and 4 and one around arms 1 and 3. This elongates the yarn in a horizontal plane.

HORIZONTAL DIAMOND SPACE WRAP: When a faster "travel" along the horizontal arms is required, three turns are taken along arms 2 and 4, and one turn around arms 1 and 3.

RELEVANT FACTS

STICKS USED: Most ojos in this book are made on wood sticks, not dowels. In using dowels, glue must be applied to back of sticks while wrapping. This is not required when using squarish sticks. The lumber is clear Douglas fir, expensive but strong. The best way to obtain these sticks is to order two 1" x 6" boards, 6' long milled into wide sticks on one board and narrow on the other. That will give you enough lumber to make many ojos and the milling charge, while high, will be more economical than charged for a single board. Practice ojos may be made on scrap lumber, but this is not advised for making those you want to keep or give for gifts.

STICK SIZES: Directions call for either narrow or wide sticks. The narrow sticks are milled to ¼" x ⅜". The wide sticks are milled to ¾" x ⅜". A little planning before cutting up for ojo projects will enable you to get the most out of each length. **ANY OJO OVER 24" IN STICK LENGTH SHOULD BE MADE OF WIDE PIECES.**

GLUE USED: Sticks should be glued together with any white household glue. Extra glue may be used to fill in notches that do not fit perfectly, or wood putty may be used. The glue used in the wrapping should be a flexible type such as Tacky.

PAINTING: Sticks may be painted with water-based or oil-based paint. They may also be stained with wood stains. It is better to paint sticks before wrapping, but they can be colored later by painting before the last few rounds of wrapping.

NOTCHING: Lay the sticks on top of each other and carefully mark for notching. Use a small hacksaw to start cut, then either with an X-Acto knife or small chisel, very carefully cut out to half the depth of the wood. Notch each piece the same, checking for fit. When notching mini ojos, tape sticks on a board and use a rat tail file to notch several at one time.

STARTING AND STOPPING
Unless otherwise directed, winding material is always glued on the back side of the ojo. Starting point is usually arm 1. Threads are **never** tied off, but are glued neatly. When changing colors, the old and new ends are pushed snugly together to avoid unwanted spacing. When wrapping dimensionals, be sure the new yarn starts in the same direction as the old finished, treating the new thread as a continuation of the old.
When adding a new color to one already being worked to make a twist wrap, it will be easier to put glue on arm, then slip new color under continuing color and press down on both yarns. Let it dry before proceeding with twist wrap.
Check carefully whenever changing colors frequently to be sure the starting and stopping is not spacing out your yarns. If the constant gluing off and on is making you go down one arm faster than you should, try tightly twisting the end to be glued to make it as small as possible.

HANGING
With a piece of matching thread, pick a place in the wrapping about 3" down the arm. Tie in snugly with a double square knot. (Go over thread twice before pulling down). Then tie loop with single finger knot, just as you knot sewing thread.
When hanging heavy ojos, attach a sawtooth hanger sideways and loop wire under the top edge of hanger.

MEASUREMENTS
THE EYE: To measure the eye, place ruler along the side of the eye, not across the center. In measuring an oblong eye, measure the long side.
THE WING: To measure the wing, place ruler along the center herringbone of the wing, measuring from the start to the point.
FLAT WRAPS: To measure either top or back wraps, measure across the threads at right angles.

SOURCES
While other types of yarn may be substituted in directions given (See page 50), it is sometimes desirable to use yarns called for to get the proper effect of the design. If you cannot find the yarn mentioned and wish to locate it, send a stamped self-addressed envelope with your query to Hunter Publishing Company as listed on the first page of the book and you will be given the sources of any materials mentioned in the directions.

MAKING ENDS NEAT

ARROWING: Make an arrow-shaped template from a piece of stiff material, such as plastic from the cover of a stationery box. Center the point carefully on sticks and cut with a small saw.

BEVELING: The ends of your sticks may be beveled by either drawing them toward you, one side at a time, on rough sandpaper, or by holding against a grinding wheel.

POMPONS: One of the quickest and easiest trims for ojos is pompons. Used on the hanging arm, they cover the hanging loop. Made of strands of the colors used in the ojo, they tend to tie the whole design together. The best way to make even pompons is to use one of the kits available in knitting shops for less than $2, with several size templates in the kit.

TASSELED POMPON: Make pompon in usual fashion. Cut 4 strands of yarn 12" long. Before tying center thread of pompon tight, pull extra strands of yarn through to center, allowing ends to dangle freely. Complete pompon fastening.
Note: To the Indians, the pompon represents a puffy cloud, symbol of the gentle life-giving rains.

FLOWER POMPONS: Using a piece of heavy cardboard, one inch wide (or a plastic pocket ruler one inch wide), wrap 26 turns of desired color around pattern. With a wool needle pull a piece of tying wool under top edge and make a double knot pulling very snugly. Cut lower edge. Holding center very tightly (use pliers if desired), with a pet brush fluff pompon, being sure brush separates each strand. Tie as for regular pompon on end of stick.

FLAT POMPONS: In trimming the top side of a mobile ojo, or sometimes on a wall-hanging ojo, a full rounded pompon is not desired. In this case, a flat pompon is made by using only ⅔ the usual amount of yarn pieces and allowing the pompon to flatten out when tied in place.

SATELLITE POMPONS: Using a pompon maker in the size called for, cut 8 pieces of yarn 10" long and pull through center of pompon maker before cutting and tying. Be sure tying goes between the dangling ends. After completing pompon, unwind the 10" pieces into single ply strands. If desired, these may be carefully brushed out with a wire pet brush.

SHRINK ART: A simple trim for special theme ojos can be made using the quick method of Shrink Art plastic on patterns in children's books, greeting cards, craft books, etc. To attach to the ojo, use a small piece of wood to give dimension and attach by gluing Shrink Art to wood piece, then glue to ojo.

BEADWORK: Most Indian stores and souvenir shops carry some beadwork on thongs for wear around neck, etc. These can be detached and used to trim the ojo eye or the stick ends. Be careful not to cut any threads that may hold beads to backing. Attach with glue.

CLOWN TASSELS: For each tassel, cut 6 pieces of yarn in desired length. (For small ojos such as FIESTA TIME IN JUAREZ, cut yarn 3" long. For larger ojos cut longer). Lay 3 pieces along each side of arm with center point against ojo point (see diagram) and tie snugly against ojo with a double strand of matching yarn. The resulting tassel resembles the fright wigs of circus clowns.

PLASTIC TIPS: Plastic tips for chair legs are available in a variety of sizes at variety, hardware and building supply stores. If possible, buy the white ones. Spray with gold paint, (being sure paint used is suitable for plastic), for fancy ojos with gold threads in the winding, or paint colors to blend with yarns used.

(Continued on page 50)

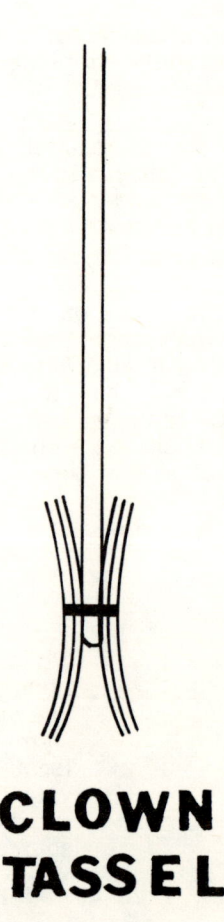

CLOWN TASSEL

CENTER TRIMS

HUICOL SUN GOD

The Huicol Indians of Southern Mexico have an art form of colored yarns used to "paint" animals and objects such as vases, boxes, wall placques, etc. The design of this Sun God is Hopi, but the work is Huicol.

MATERIAL:
One 3½" round wood placque no thicker than ⅜". These may be obtained in most craft shops.
Two yards of each color of rug yarn will be more than sufficient.

PROCEDURE:
Draw a guide line across center of placque. Glue black yarn in two rows along line. Glue two rows of black yarn vertically from center to upper edge. When dry, fill in right-hand quarter-circle with green yarn by gluing pieces along black lines. Repeat with orange yarn in left quarter-circle.

Working horizontally, glue one piece of cream yarn below black line. Cut six pieces of black yarn ¼" long. Following diagram, glue eyes in position using two of the pieces for each eye. Fill in around eyes with cream yarn working horizontally. Glue four more cream pieces across placque. Using last two pieces of black, place mouth in center. Finish covering placque with cream yarn.

Glue three rows of rust yarn around edge covering ends. Trim any ends that may show.

Placing 3 colors of feathers close together, glue to the back of the placque so they extend 2" beyond edge.

COLORS:
Orange rug yarn
Green rug yarn
Black rug yarn
Cream rug yarn
Rust rug yarn

DOUGHBREAD KACHINA

Another different center trim can be made in the popular craft of bread dough. This very old European art form can be easily done by mixing 1 cup of all purpose flour with ½ cup of table salt. After mixing well, add ½ cup water a little at a time. Do not make the dough too sticky, yet it must be flexible enough to mold with the fingers.

After making your design to suit, bake in a pre-heated oven at 325° until surface is light brown. You may bake it on a Teflon pan for easy cleaning, or by lining a cookie sheet with cooking foil SHINY SIDE UP. Foil increases oven heat, so you may have to turn your oven to 300°.

For the Kachina, you will need a 3½" high table salt shaker of cardboard. Remove the plastic top, turn upside down. On shaker bottom, crumple a nicely rounded ball of foil to form head.

Flouring your hands, the roller and a piece of foil, roll out the dough to no more than ½" thick piece. Laying the shaker on a firm surface, flatten on back with careful pressure, being sure front remains rounded. Cut a circle of dough 3½" in diameter and drape evenly over head. Cut a rectangular piece of dough 3" wide and long enough to wrap around body. With moistened fingers, press head and body pieces together. Where they join, attach a small rolled piece around the box. Cut two small arched pieces for ears and attach with water to sides of head. With two rolled pieces 1½" long, shape two legs and feet and attach at bottom inside edge of lower skirt. Last, attach a small rolled piece for the nose.

When cool, paint as desired with acrylic paints and glue feathers on top of head. Glue to ojo center.

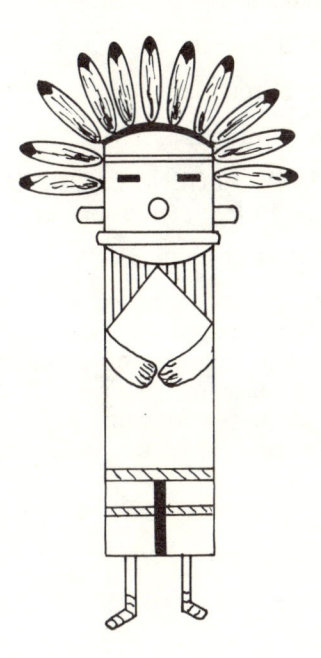

ALOHA LEI

When arriving in our 50th State, the visitor is usually greeted with a lei of flowers. The floral necklace ojo appears to be suspended in air when hung on a wall. The flower names are Hawaii's special flora.

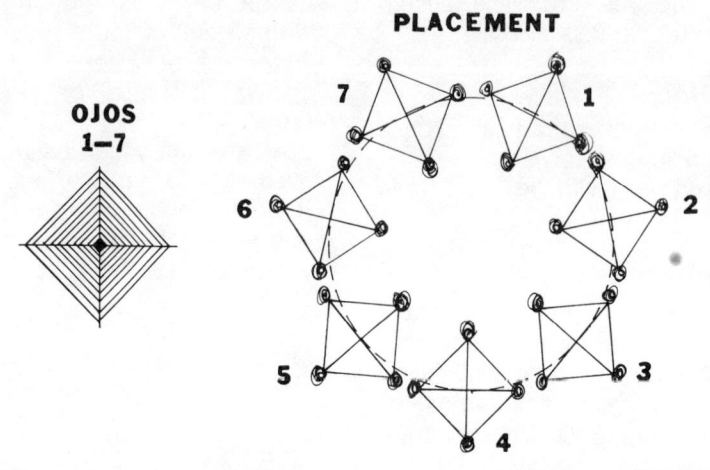

PLACEMENT

OJOS 1–7

STICKS:
Cut fourteen 5½" sticks from fireplace matches. (⅛" dowels may be substituted but if used a line of glue must be run along each arm to keep wool from slipping.)

NOTCHING:
Notch each stick in center. Leave sticks unpainted and ends unfinished.

GLUING:
Glue sticks into seven basic mini ojos.

PROCEDURE:
With color 1 make an eye of 5 rounds.

With color 2 do 3 rounds.

With color 3 do 5 rounds.

With color 4 do 4 rounds.

TAKING TWO WRAPS AROUND EACH ARM, do 2 rounds of color 2, change to back wrap and do 4 more rounds.

Finish with 4 rounds of color 3.

Trim with flower pompons in color 2. (See MAKING ENDS NEAT). Using diagram below attach each ojo in place on a 14" ring. This may be a colored plastic embroidery hoop or a macrame ring wound in four ply yarn. Use epoxy glue to fasten ojos on ring.

COLOR CHART:
(Yarn used is Persian 2-ply, color numbers from DMC)

Plumeria (Ojo 1)
1. Marigold 7436
2. Dark orange 7439
3. Dark cream 7745
4. Lemon 7726

Shower Tree (Ojo 2)
1. Soft green 7768
2. Light green 7771
3. Moss green 7377
4. Lemon 7434

Anthurium (Ojo 3)
1. Deep rose 7603
2. Light rose 7605
3. Raspberry 7600
4. Pink 7134

Silver Sword (Ojo 4)
1. Dark blue 7797
2. Robin's egg blue 7599
3. Medium blue 7798
4. Soft blue 7799

Pikake (Ojo 5)
1. Dark gold 7444
2. Ecru 7453
3. Apricot 7437
4. Yellow 7742

Poinsettia (Ojo 6)
1. Peach 7851
2. Light peach 7852
3. Light coral 7850
4. Red coral 7606

Croton (Ojo 7)
1. Emerald 7943
2. Lime 7954
3. Forest green 7329
4. Medium green 7912

MAUI WOOD ROSE

Hawaii's most unusual flower is the Wood Rose, a growing plant whose rose blossoms shade from golden tan to deep brown. When the flower dries it does not wither but lasts for years if handled properly. The texture resembles fine wood shavings.

STICKS:
Cut two 12" and two 24" sticks in narrow width.

NOTCHING:
Notch each stick in center. Bevel ends.

GLUING:
Glue each pair of sticks into a basic ojo. When dry lay the 12" ojo on top spacing arms evenly, drill a 3/32" hole in center and fasten together with a small brass screw, tightening with nut. Cut off any excess. Paint sticks chocolate brown.

PROCEDURE:
Numbering the 12" sticks 1, 2, 3, 4 and the 24" sticks 5, 6, 7, 8, attach color 1 on arm 1 and working only arms 1, 2, 3, 4, make a 1¾" eye.

With color 1 on arm 5 back wrap working only arms 5, 6, 7, 8 for 1¼" from center of screw.

Attach color 2 on arm 4. Wing wrap arms 4 and 2 for ½". Attach color 2 on arm 3. Wing wrap arms 3 and 1 for ½". Attach color 2 on arm 5. Taking 2 turns, wing wrap arms 5 and 7 for 1". Attach color 2 on arm 8. Taking 2 turns, wing wrap arms 8 and 6 for 1".

Attach color 3 on arm 1. Wing wrap arms 1 and 3 for ½". Attach color 3 on arm 2. Wing wrap arms 2 and 4 for ½". Attach color 3 on arm 6. Taking 2 turns, wing wrap arms 6 and 8 for 1". Attach color 3 on arm 7. Taking 2 turns, wing wrap arms 7 and 5 for 1".

Attach color 4 on arm 3. Wing wrap arms 3 and 1 for ½". Attach color 4 on arm 4. Wing wrap arms 4 and 2 for ½". Attach color 4 on arm 8. Taking 2 turns, wing wrap arms 8 and 6 for 1". Attach color 4 on arm 5. Taking 2 turns, wing wrap arms 5 and 7 for 1".

Attach color 5 on arm 1. Wing wrap arms 1 and 3 for ½". Attach color 5 on arm 2. Wing wrap arms 2 and 4 for ½". Attach color 5 on arm 6. Taking 2 turns, wing wrap arms 6 and 8 for 1". Attach color 5 on arm 7. Taking 2 turns, wing wrap arms 7 and 5 for 1".

Attach color 6 on arm 3. Wing wrap arms 3 and 1 for ½". Attach color 6 on arm 4. Wing wrap arms 4 and 2 for ½". Attach color 6 on arm 8. Taking 2 turns, wing wrap arms 8 and 6 for 1". Attach color 6 on arm 5. Taking 2 turns, wing wrap arms 5 and 7 for 1".

Attach color 7 on arm 1. Wing wrap arms 1 and 3 for ½". Attach color 7 on arm 2. Wing wrap arms 2 and 4 for ½". Attach color 7 on arm 6. Taking 2 turns, wing wrap arms 6 and 8 for 1¼". Attach color 7 on arm 7. Taking 2 turns, wing wrap arms 7 and 5 for 1¼".

With color 1 extend wrap arms 5, 6, 7, 8 for 2¼", being sure to start with the same place on yarn color so arms will match. Do not cut yarn on last arm (arm 8).

Taking one turn around arms 1, 2, 3, 4 and 2 turns around arms 5, 6, 7, 8, top wrap for 5 rounds. Keep tension very tight so yarn will not slip off shorter arms. Do not cut off.

Taking only one turn on each arm, top wrap for 2 rounds and glue off. Put a small amount of glue on the last wrap of arms 1, 2, 3, 4 to assure holding.

Hang either by arm 6 as pictured or by arm 3 if desired.

COLORS:
1. Variegated "Navaho" (shades of brown, cream, orange.)
2. Cream
3. Light gold
4. Medium gold
5. Dark gold
6. Light brown
7. Dark brown

HAWAIIAN ORCHID

STICKS:

Cut four 18" sticks in narrow width.

NOTCHING:

Notch each stick in center. Bevel ends.

GLUING:

Glue into two basic ojos. When dry drill a small hole through the centers and fasten together with a brass screw, 3/32", being sure spacing is equal. Tighten with a nut and cut off any excess. Paint sticks purple.

PROCEDURE:

Attach color 1 on arm 1 and working only on arms 1, 2, 3, 4 do a ¾" eye.

Attach color 1 on arm 5 and back wrap working only on arms 5, 6, 7, 8 until wrapping measures ¾" from center back of screw (about 10 rounds).

Attach color 2 on arm 3. Top wrap in rotation arms 4, 1, 2 and 3 for 3 rounds. Attach color 3 on arm 1 and do 3 rounds.

Attach color 4 on arm 7. Top wrapping only arms 7, 8, 5 and 6 (passing under other arms) do 5 rounds. Attach color 2 on arm 3 and working only arms 4, 1, 2 and 3 top wrap 2 rounds. Attach color 1 on arm 1. Working only arms 1, 2, 3, 4 do 3 rounds.

Attach color 2 on arm 5 and wrapping only arms 5, 6, 7, 8, (passing under other arms) do 9 rounds.

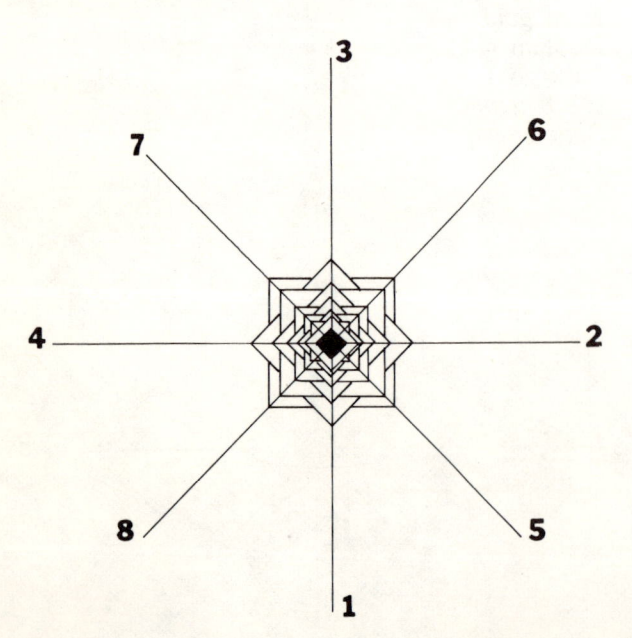

From now on entire ojo is star wrapped (See TERMINOLOGY).

Attach color 5 on arm 2. Star wrap arms 2, 3, 4, 1 for 5 rounds. Attach color 3 on arm 1. Star wrap arms 1, 2, 3 4 for 3 rounds.

Taking 2 turns around every arm from now on work as follows: Attach color 2 on arm 6. Star wrap arms 7, 8, 5, 6 for 6 rounds. Attach color 2 on arm 3. Star wrap arms 3, 4, 1, 2 for 4 rounds. Attach color 2 on arm 7. Star wrap arms 7, 8, 5, 6 for 6 rounds. Attach color 1 on arm 4. Star wrap arms 4, 1, 2, 3 for 6 rounds. Attach color 2 on arm 5. Star wrap arms 6, 7, 8, 5 for 6 rounds. Attach color 2 on arm 3. Star wrap arms 3, 4, 1, 2 for 6 rounds. Attach color 4 on arm 7. Star wrap arms 7, 8, 5, 6 for 6 rounds.

Attach color 2 on arm 1. Star wrap arms 1, 2, 3, 4 for 6 rounds. Attach color 5 on arm 6. Star wrap arms 6, 7, 8, 5 for 6 rounds. Attach color 2 on arm 4. Star wrap arms 4, 1, 2, 3 for 6 rounds. Attach color 3 on arm 8. Star wrap arms 8, 5, 6, 7 for 6 rounds. Attach color 2 on arm 2. Star wrap arms 2, 3, 4, 1 for 6 rounds. Attach color 4 on arm 6. Star wrap arms 6, 7, 8, 5 for 6 rounds. Attach color 2 on arm 4. Star wrap arms 4, 1, 2, 3 for 6 rounds.

Taking only one turn on each arm, attach color 1 on arm 1, and star wrap arms 1, 2, 3, 4 for 4 rounds. Without gluing off add color 3 and do 1 round of twist wrap (See TERMINOLOGY). Glue off color 3 but continue star wrapping with color 1 for 2 more rounds, taking 2 turns on each arm.

Taking only one turn on each arm, attach color 1 on arm 5 and star wrap arms 5, 6, 7, 8 for 4 rounds. Without gluing off, add color 3 and do one round of twist wrap. Glue off color 3 but continue star wrapping with color 1 for two more rounds, taking 2 turns on each arm.

COLORS:

1. Deep purple
2. Light pink
3. Red sparkle
4. Variegated purple shades
5. Medium lavendar

PELE'S COMET

Pele is the goddess of fire in Hawaii. When the volcanoes erupt, Pele is showing her displeasure. In olden times live sacrifices were made to stop the fiery chunks of lava that were ejected trailing fiery tails. The bamboo hoops used to trim this ojo are common to Hawaii.

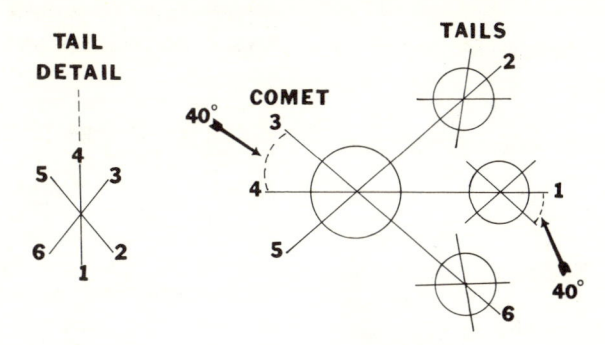

STICKS:
Cut three 24", six 8" sticks in narrow width.

NOTCHING:
Laying on template, notch two 8" sticks to fit 40° angle, 4" up from end of 24" stick. Make all three sticks the same way.

GLUING:
Glue 8" sticks in place to make 3 separate ojos. (The 24" sticks will not be worked until all the shorter ones are done.) Paint bright yellow.

PROCEDURE:
TAILS

With color 1, do an oblong eye for 1¼". (See TERMINOLOGY and HOW TO MEASURE).

On arm 1, attach color 2 and Oblong Star Wrap (See TERMINOLOGY) by going over and around arm 1, under arm 2, over and around arm 3, under arm 4, over and around arm 5, under arm 6. Do 5 rounds.

Attach color 3 on arm 2. Oblong Star Wrap by going over and around arm 2, under arm 3, over and around arm 4, under arm 5, over and around arm 6, under arm 1. Do 5 rounds.

Attach color 4 on arm 6. Do Figure 8 weave by going over and around arm 6, under and around arm 1, over and around arm 2 with 1½ turns, over and around arm 1, under and around arm 6 with 1½ turns. Do 4 complete rounds and glue off on arm 6.

Attach color 5 on arm 3. Do Figure 8 weave by going over and around arm 3, under and around arm 4, over and around arm 5 with 1½ turns, over and around arm 4, under and around arm 3 with 1½ turns. Do 4 complete rounds and glue off on arm 3.

Attach color 6 on arm 1. Back wrap each arm for 8 rounds (about ⅜").

Make other two tails to match.

COMET
Lay three 24" sticks on template and notch at 40° angle 8" from ends of sticks. Glue in place.
With color 1 on arm 4, do an oblong eye of 1½".
Attach color 3 on arm 3. Oblong Star Wrap on arms 3, 5 and 1 for 6 rounds. Attach color 5 on arm 4. Oblong Star Wrap on arms 4, 6 and 2 for 6 rounds.
With color 2 on arm 3, Figure 8 wrap following pattern for comet tails for 4 complete rounds. With color 2 on arm 6, Figure 8 wrap for 4 complete rounds.
With color 3 on arm 3, Figure 8 wrap for 3 complete rounds. With color 3 on arm 6, Figure 8 wrap for 3 complete rounds.
With color 4 on arm 1, backwrap for 6 rounds. With color 5 on arm 6, backwrap for 3 rounds. With color 6 on arm 6, backwrap for 3 rounds.
Attach color 2 on arm 3. Figure 8 wrap for 3 complete rounds. Attach color 2 on arm 6 and Figure 8 wrap for 3 rounds. Attach color 3 on arm 3 and Figure 8 wrap for 3 rounds. Attach color 3 on arm 6 and Figure 8 wrap for 3 rounds.

TAKING 2 TURNS AROUND EACH ARM, attach color 6 on arm 3 and backwrap for 4 rounds. Attach color 5 to arm 6. Top wrap for 4 rounds, change to back wrap and do 3 rounds. Attach color 4 on arm 3, do 4 rounds in back wrap.

FINISHING:
Using one 9" and three 5" bamboo hoops obtainable in craft stores, paint hoops bright red. (If hoops are in burnt finish, they may be left unpainted if desired.)
Lay small hoops over tails, checking for even spacing, and large hoop over comet. Glue in place.

COLORS:
1. Red
2. Yellow
3. Light orange
4. Rust
5. Ivory
6. Reddish orange boucle

KANEHOE

In Hawaiian, Kanehoe means 'skinny man'.

STICKS:
Cut one 48" and four 12" sticks in narrow width.

NOTCHING:
Notch 12" sticks in center. Notch 48" stick at 18" and 42" up from end.

GLUING:
Glue two of the 12" sticks into a basic ojo. Glue one 12" stick at 42" notch of 48" stick and reserve the last 12" stick until later. Bevel all ends. Paint sticks blue.

PROCEDURE:
Place the 12" basic ojo on top of the 48" stick at the 42" notch and fasten by drilling a small hole through the center and inserting a brass screw. Tighten with a nut, being sure to space arms evenly.

HEAD:
Attach color 1 on arm 5 and do a rosebud eye (See TERMINOLOGY).
Attach color 2 on arm 3 and back wrap for 5 rounds.
Attach color 3 on arm 1 and back wrap for 4 rounds.
Attach color 4 on arm 3 and top wrap for 3 rounds.
Attach color 5 on arm 1 and top wrap for 2 rounds.

PATTERN A:
Attach color 2 on arm 8. Triple figure 8 wrap by going over arm 8, under and around arm 1, over and around arm 5 with 1½ turns, over and around arm 1, under and around arm 8 with 1½ turns. Do two complete rounds.

PATTERN B:
Attach color 2 on arm 6. Triple figure eight wrap by going over arm 6, under and around arm 3, over and around arm 7 with 1½ turns, over and around arm 3, under and around arm 6 with 1½ turns. Do two rounds.
Attach color 1 on arm 8. Repeat Triple figure eight pattern A for 3 complete rounds. Attach color 1 on arm 6. Repeat Triple figure eight pattern B for 3 complete rounds.

Attach color 6 on arm 2. Extend wrap for 1". Glue off.
Attach color 6 on arm 4. Extend wrap for 1". Do not glue off. Top wrap each arm in sequence for 5 rounds.
Attach color 7 on arm 8. Top wrap for 2 rounds. Without gluing off change to back wrap and do 6 rounds.
Attach color 3 on arm 3 and back wrap for 2 rounds.
Attach color 4 on arm 1 and back wrap for 2 rounds. Do not glue off.

Change to Multiple figure eight wrap by going * over and around arm 5, under and around arm 2, over and around arm 6, under and around arm 3, over and around arm 7, under and around arm 4, over and around arm 8, over and around arm 1, under and around arm 5, over and around arm 2, under and around arm 6, over and around arm 3, under and around arm 7, over and around arm 4, under and around arm 8, over and around arm 1.

Repeat from * twice.

Attach color 3 on arm 5. Back wrap for 4 rounds.

BODY:
Glue last 12" stick at 18" notch.

Attach color 7 on arm 9. Wrap a diamond eye (See TERMINOLOGY) until it measures 1".

From now on, space diamond wrap by taking 3 turns around arms 1 and 3, and one turn around arms 9 and 10. Attach color 2 on arm 10 and do 4 rounds. Attach color 6 to arm 9 and do 7 rounds. Attach color 4 to arm 10 and do 3 rounds.

Taking only 1 turn around each arm, attach color 3 to arm 10 and do 2 rounds.

COLORS:
1. Rose
2. Ivory
3. Unger #9 or similar bouclé in green/white
4. Coral
5. Gray
6. Faded blue denim
7. Teal tweed

KANEHOE (Cont.)

Attach color 7 on arm 1. Wing wrap arms 1 and 3 taking 2 turns around each arm, for 1¼" (See HOW TO MEASURE). Be sure threads lie flat. (See HELPFUL HINTS.) Attach color 2 on arm 1. Taking 1 turn around each arm, outline wing wrap with 2 rounds.

Taking 1 turn around arms 9 and 10 and 3 turns around arms 1 and 3, attach color 1 on arm 10 and wrap for 5 rounds. Attach color 2 on arm 9 and do 3 rounds.

Attach color 5 on arm 10 and extend wrap 10 rounds. Without gluing off, extend wrap arm 3 for 10 rounds. Without gluing off, extend wrap arm 9 for 10 rounds. Without gluing off, extend wrap arm 1 for 10 rounds and glue off on arm 10 by tucking behind beginning extend wrap.

Attach color 4 on arm 10. Wrap over arm 10, * under and around arm 3 with 3 turns, over and around arm 9 with 1½ turns, over and around arm 3 with 3 turns, under and around arm 10 with 1½ turns. Repeat from * twice.

Attach color 7 to arm 9. Tree wrap by going ** over arm 1 with 3 turns, over and around arm 10 with 1½ turns, over arm 1 with 3 turns, over and around arm 9 with 1½ turns. Repeat from ** twice.

Attach color 3 on arm 10. Taking 1 wrap on each arm, top wrap for 1 round. Attach color 6 on arm 1. Extend wrap 3". Attach color 6 on arm 3. Extend wrap 3". Fasten with glue but do not cut. Taking 3 turns around arms 1 and 3 only, do 10 rounds. Taking 1 turn around each arm do 1 round. Do not glue off. Extend wrap arm 3 to meet HEAD ojo.

BOW TIE:

Glue two 4½" popsicle sticks (available in craft stores) together at the center at a 20° angle, using template. Paint medium green.

Attach color 1 on arm 1.
Figure eight wrap over arm 1, * under and over arm 2, under and over arm 1. Repeat from * for a total of 6 rounds.

Work arms 3 and 4 to match. (Center will remain unwrapped.)

With color 4, do 10 rounds on each pair of arms following figure eight pattern. With color 3, do 2 rounds.

With color 6, wrap over the center until fully covered, working from the center out along each pair of arms. Glue bow tie below head.

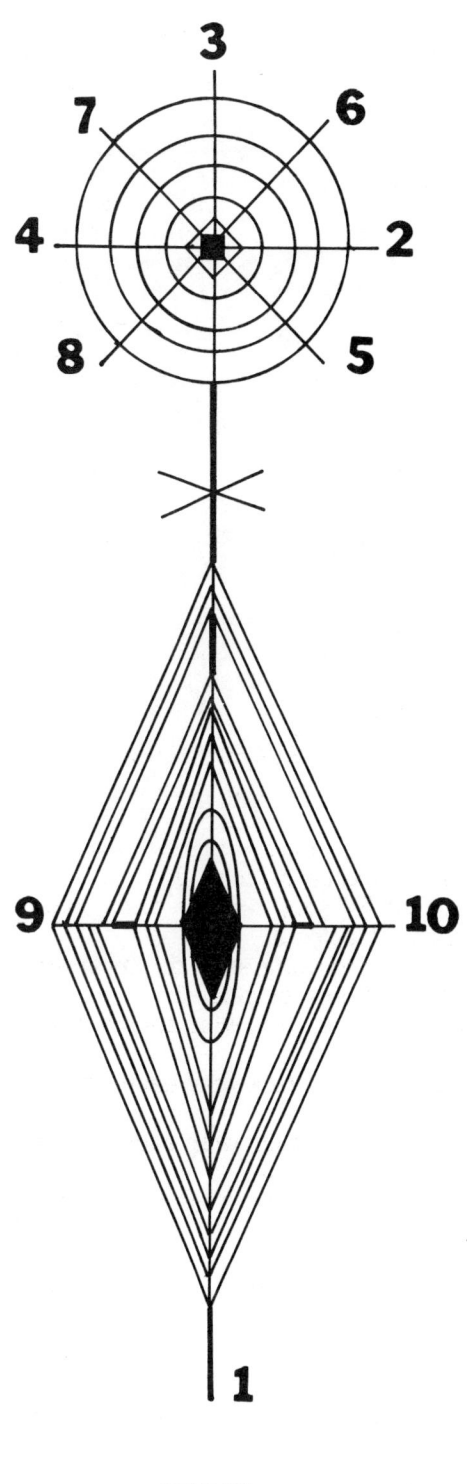

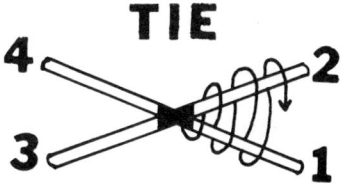

CONCHA

In the prehistoric jewelry of the Hohokam Indians, the "early ones" who lived in Arizona and vanished around 1250, shells were used as bracelets and pendants, or put together with thongs to make belts. Bits of coral and turquoise were often imbedded in the shells to form mosaic patterns. The shells were often black mother-of-pearl obtained by the Hohokams who lived in the Gila River and Salt River areas of Arizona by trading with Indians from Baja California who found the conchas on the beaches of the Gulf of California as well as the Pacific Ocean. The pink, white and black colors of this ojo reflect the colors of the ancient shell jewelry pieces. The silver represents the later use of metal in their jewelry.

STICKS:
Cut one 36", and three 16" sticks in narrow width.

NOTCHING:
Notch 36" stick at 10½", 18", and 25½" up. Notch 16" sticks in the center. Bevel all ends.

GLUING:
Glue a 16" stick at each notch on the 36" stick. Paint with two coats of silver spray paint finishing with one coat of clear plastic.

PROCEDURE:
With color 1, make a 1¼" eye at each cross. Outline with 1 round of color 6.
With color 2, do ½" wing wrap on upper arms 1 and 5. Outline with 3 rounds of color 3.
With color 2, do ½" wing wrap on arms 3 and 7. Outline with 3 rounds of color 3.
With color 2, do ½" wing wrap on lower arms 1 and 5. Outline with 3 rounds of color 3.
With color 4 on arm 1, back wrap each arm in succession for 5 rounds.
With color 5 on arm 1, back wrap each arm in succession for 3 rounds.
With color 1 on arm 1, back wrap each arm in succession for 4 rounds.
DO NOT CUT OFF, change to top wrap and do 4 rounds.
Working all in top wrap:
With color 6 do 3 rounds.
With color 3 do 2 rounds.
With color 7 do 4 rounds.
With color 4 do 4 rounds.
With color 7 do 3 rounds.
TAKING TWO TURNS ON ARMS 1 and 5, 1 turn on balance of arms:
With color 8 do 3 rounds.
With color 2 do 3 rounds.
With color 1 do 5 rounds.
With color 3 do 2 rounds.
With color 5 do 3 rounds.
With color 1 do 4 rounds.
With color 6 do 4 rounds.
Taking 1 turn around each arm, with color 3 do 4 rounds.
Hang by arm 3.

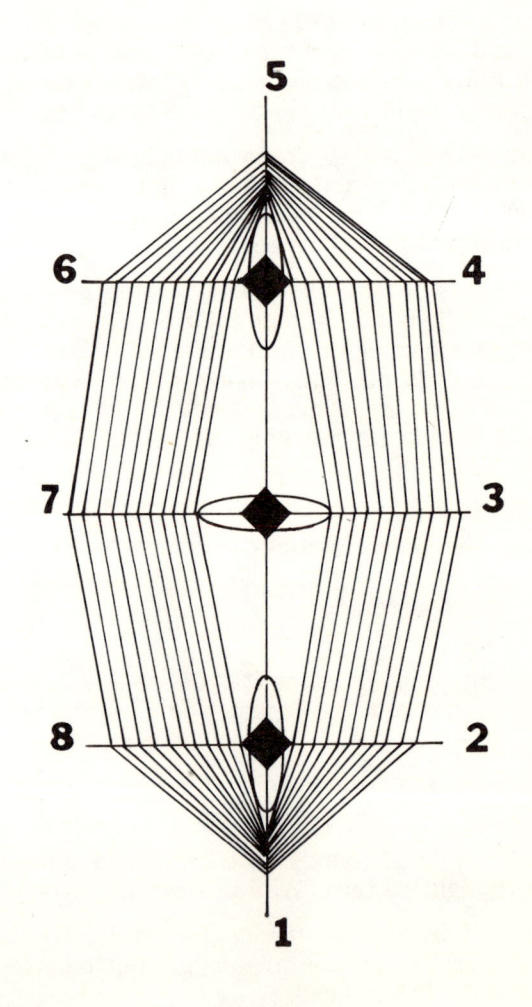

COLORS:
1. Black
2. Pink
3. Rose boucle
4. Variegated in gray/white/black
5. Pink Madison (from Israel)
6. Silver Bucilla Brocade
7. White and silver Soirée (from France)
8. Coral

CHRISTMAS IN ARIZONA

The directions given use a piece of cholla cactus wood available in desert regions. Any attractive gnarled wood, or piece of beach driftwood may be substituted.

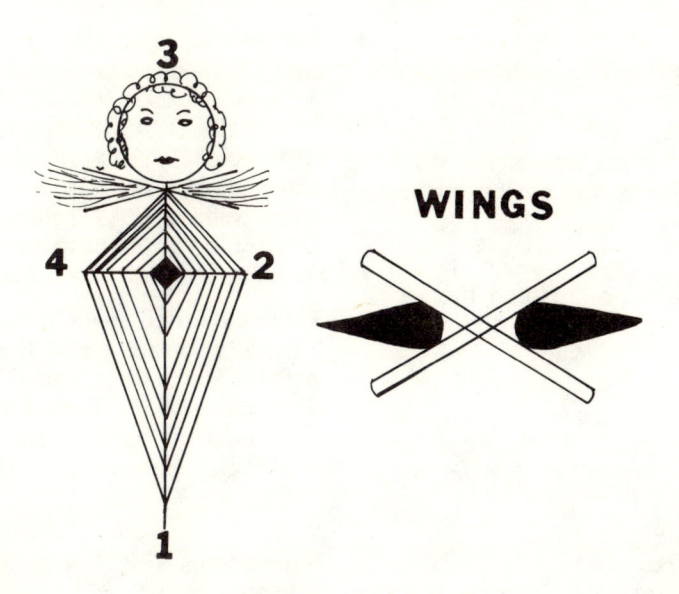

STICKS:
Using barbeque sticks, (available in gourmet and Oriental import shops) cut six 5¼" long, six 4" long, and twelve 3" long.

NOTCHING:
Notch the 5¼" sticks 2" down from top. Notch 4" sticks in center. Notch the 12 remaining sticks for a 60° angle at center, using a template. Be careful to make shallow notches using a rat tail file.

GLUING:
Glue the 4" sticks at the 2" notch to form a cross. Glue the remaining 12 sticks at 60° angle.

PROCEDURE:
Working on the crosses for the angel body do a ⅝" eye in color 1. With color 2 do 3 rounds. Do not cut yarn.

Begin space wrap with 1 turn around arms 2, 3, 4, and 2 turns on arm 1 for 8 rounds. Now taking 2 turns on arms 2, 3, 4 and 3 turns on arm 1, do 6 rounds.

With color 3 using same space wrap do 1 round. With color 1, using only 2 turns on arms 2 and 4, 1 turn on arm 3, and 3 turns on arm 1, do 2 rounds. With color 2, follow same wrap for 2 rounds.

Taking 1 turn around each arm, do 1 round of color 3.

FINISHING:
Insert arm 3 into a plastic angel head, available in craft shops, and glue securely.

Wings may be made in a variety of ways. You may glue feathers to the 12 angled pieces, or you may gather a piece of white nylon tulle, 6" wide and 15" long through the center and tie at angle crossing.

A most effective wing is made by fastening two tear-drop pendants (used for craft lamp making) together at wide end with a piece of 30 gauge florist wire. This in turn should be wired to the angled sticks and the gathered tulle fastened in the center.

With crystal nylon thread of varying lengths, fasten angels to the wood support. This is best done by attaching the thread to the top of the angels head so they swing upright. Using 5 clusters of plastic greenery (picks) fasten greenery to top of wood. If desired add an ornament star just below wood and higher than the angels.

Hang with a green velvet rope or with wire.

COLORS:
Using white as color 2 and Bucilla gold brocade as color 3, color 1 will be red, teal, green, purple, orange, and aqua, a different color for each angel.

NAVAHO BRAVE

A traditional Indian ojo in Navaho rug colors. The prayer stick ends feature the bells and black and white plumes used during the ceremonial Navaho dances.

STICKS:
Cut one 48", one 36", and two 32" sticks in wide width.

NOTCHING:
On this ojo the notching is done on the side of the stick, not the flat. This gives dimension to the ojo by raising one above the other.

Notch the 32" stick in the center, on the sides. Notch the 36" stick in the center on the side. Notch the 48" stick in the center on the side and bevel one end. This will be arm 5.

GLUING:
Glue the 32" sticks into a basic ojo. Glue the other two sticks into an elongated ojo with the 48" stick being the vertical. Paint black.

PROCEDURE:
On both ojos with color 1 do a 1¾" eye. With color 2 do matching ¾" wing wraps on each ojo.

Placing ojos on top of one another with the 48" stick on top of the 32" ojo, and spacing evenly, wrap every arm with color 3 for 8 rounds. Check on template to be sure spacing has stayed even. With color 4 do 3 rounds, with color 5 do 2 rounds, with color 1 do 9 rounds.

Taking two turns around arms, glue color 2 on arm 2. Star wrap (See TERMINOLOGY) by going under arm 3, over arm 4, under arm 5, over arm 6, under arm 7, over arm 8, under arm 1, and returning over arm 2 for 11 rounds.

Glue color 3 on arm 1 and star wrap, taking 2 turns only on arms 1 and 5, by going under arm 2, over arm 3, under arm 4, over arm 5, under arm 6, over arm 7, under arm 8, and returning over arm 1 for 9 rounds. **Do not glue off.** Taking 3 turns on arms 1 and 5, and 2 turns on arms 3 and 7, continue in same star wrap for 5 rounds. Following same pattern do 4 rounds of color 5.

At this point, winding should measure 5" from center of eye on arms 2, 3, 4, 6, and 8, and 6" on arms 1 and 5. Adjust windings if necessary.

With color 4 on arm 1 repeat same star pattern for 3 rounds. **Do not cut yarn.** Extend wrap 1¼" down arm 1. Do not cut off, but go to arm 3, passing under arm 2, and extend wrap 1¼" down arm 3. Without cutting off go to arm 5, passing under arm 4 and extend wrap 1¼". Without cutting off go to arm 7, passing under arm 6, and extend wrap 1¼". Do not cut off but passing under arm 8, glue thread carefully around arm 1 at the **beginning** of extend wrap. Glue off.

With color 2 wrap every arm for 8 rounds starting with arm 1.

Taking 3 turns on arms 1 and 5, 2 turns on arms 3 and 7, and 1 turn on arms 2, 4, 6 and 8:
With color 3 do 4 rounds.
With color 1 do 4 rounds.
With color 5 do 4 rounds.
With color 4 do 6 rounds.
With color 2 do 7 rounds.
With color 1 do 5 rounds.
With color 3 do 6 rounds.

Begin extended space wrap with 4 turns on arms 1 and 5, 2 turns on arms 3 and 7, and 1 turn on arms 2, 4, 6, 8:
With color 5 do 4 rounds.
With color 2 do 7 rounds.
With color 4 do 3 rounds.
With color 3 do 4 rounds.

FINISHING:
Finish arms 1, 2, 3, 4, 6, 7, 8 with prayer stick feathers. Hang by arm 5.

COLORS:
1. Black
2. Variegated red/white/navy
3. Fire engine red
4. White Wintuk
5. Medium gray

NAVAHO BRAVE (Cont.)

PRAYER STICK FEATHERS:

This type of making ends neat, can be quite formal according to the fabric used (See PARTY TIME), or casual using such fabrics as felt, or leatherette. The method of making this type of trim can be a simple gathering of the material circle, tying with a bit of yarn, or decorating with clusters of feathers, beads, or other accents. The number of circles required depends on the arms to be trimmed. For Navaho Brave you will need seven prayer stick assemblies.

METHOD:

Cut seven 6" circles of red "Slicker" used in making children's rain coats and available in fabric shops. Folding in fourths with wrong side out, mark center. Opening the circle, make two quarter-inch slits, one on each side of center dot and one half-inch apart.

Cut seven white felt thongs 7" long and 3/8" wide.

Cluster 3 feathers, 2 white and 1 black, together. Hold in place by wrapping a small piece of masking tape around quill ends.

Double a felt thong and lay a cut end on top and bottom side of quills. Starting 1" below quill ends wrap quills closely with yarn in color 2. Fasten at top end with a double half hitch. (About 2" of felt thong will be left). Thread a tapestry needle with the yarn end and run under wrapping to the beginning, bringing up on the right side. Run needle through top of small bell, tack into place. Run needle under wrapping about 1/4" away and fasten second bell in same manner. Trim ends. Cut felt loop in half.

Working from the right side of the circle, pull ends of thong through slits to the wrong side.

Place center of circle, wrong side, against arm end. With a small amount of glue on top and bottom of arm fasten 1" of thong to arm. (Be sure bells are on top). Let dry. Trim off unglued ends.

Gather circle evenly around arm and tie snugly 1" from end with 3 wrappings of yarn in color 3. Knot at the back of the arm and trim. Adjust gathers so circle flares evenly.

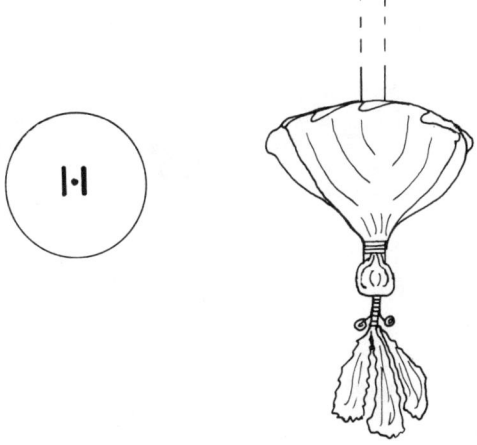

SIX FLAGS OVER TEXAS

Flags of six different countries have flown over Texas. This ojo is symbolic of the various rulers who directed what is now the State of Texas, crowned at the top by the current U.S. flag.

FLAG 1:
The Republic of Texas. Discontented with Mexican rule, by 1826 Texans attempted to obtain justice from the Mexican government. It took 10 years of protest and finally a war that lasted six months and included the tragedy of the Alamo to make Texas an independent Republic on April 21, 1836.

STAR: Glue two 8" sticks into a basic ojo. With color 1 do a 1" eye. Without cutting off start wing wrap for ¾" on arms 1 and 3. Make a matching ¾" wing wrap on arms 2 and 4. Repeat wing wraps once more, making a total of 1½" from point of eye. Lay the star aside until complete ojo is finished.

With color 2, on arm 1 of the 48" assembly, top wrap an eye for 4".
With color 3, back wrap 7 rounds. With color 4, back wrap 7 rounds.

Taking two turns around each arm, with color 3 back wrap 7 rounds. With color 4 back wrap for 6 rounds.

Taking one turn around each arm, do one more round of color 4.

FLAG 2:
The Spanish flag. The arms of Castile and Leon were combined in the Spanish flag of 1682, when two Spanish missions were built in Texas near today's city of El Paso. The flag was quartered into two opposing white fields and red fields. The upper left and lower right quarters had a gold castle while the lower left and upper right quarters had a red lion. This flag had been carried to the new world by Columbus in 1492.

Glue one 12" stick at left hand notch of 36" stick. With color 5 do a ¾" eye.

With color 4 on arm 1 in regular gluing position, and color 6 directly below it in opposite gluing position, begin double color wrap (See TERMINOLOGY) for 7 patterns. Twist threads to reverse colors and do 7 more patterns.

Taking two turns around each arm, with color 7 top wrap for 5 rounds. With color 5 do 3 rounds and with color 7 do 5 rounds.
Attach colors 4 and 6 for double-color weave and do 6 patterns. Twist threads to reverse colors and do 6 more patterns.

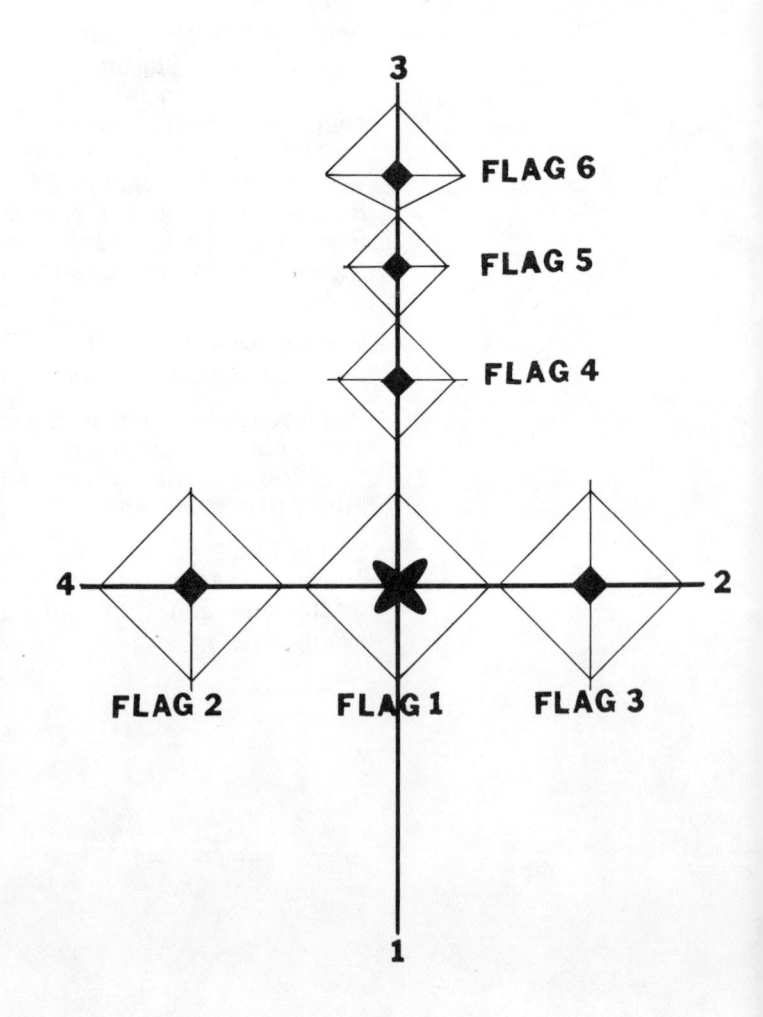

STICKS:
Cut one 48", one 36", two 12", four 8", and one 6" stick in narrow width.

NOTCHING:
Notch the 36" stick in the center and 6½" in from each end. Notch the 48" stick 5½" down, 11¼" down, 16¾" down, and 28" down from top. Notch the balance of the sticks in the center. Bevel all ends and paint all sticks white.

GLUING:
The sticks will be glued on as you work each ojo to facilitate winding. Glue the 36" stick at center notch to the 48" stick at the 28" notch.

20

SIX FLAGS OVER TEXAS (Cont.)

FLAG 3:
The French flag. In 1685, the first French settlement, Ft. St. Louis, was established on the Texas coast. At this time the French flag was a white banner with gold fleur-de-lis patterns, occasionally trimmed with blue fringe.

Glue a 12" stick at the right hand notch of the 36" stick. With color 10 do a ¾" eye. With color 6 do 5 rounds.

Taking two turns on each arm, with color 7 do 5 rounds.

Attaching color 10 above and color 5 below, do a double color wrap for 3 patterns. Twist threads to reverse colors and do 3 more patterns.

With color 2 back wrap 4 rounds.
With color 7 top wrap for 6 rounds.

Taking two turns around each arm, with color 11 top wrap for 3 rounds. With color 5 do 2 rounds. With color 10 do 5 rounds. With color 5 do 3 rounds.
Taking only 1 turn around each arm do 4 rounds of color 7. Taking 2 wraps around each arm do 2 rounds of color 2. Taking 1 wrap around each arm do 2 rounds of color 2.

FLAG 4:
The Confederate flag. In 1861 Texas seceded from the Union and for nine years was a Confederate state. The adopted flag had seven stars in a ring, representing the seven seceding states, on a blue field. There were three stripes horizontally, a white stripe in the center of two red ones. Texas troops refused to carry the flag into battle as it resembled the U.S. flag too closely.

Glue an 8" stick at the 16¾" notch.
With color 4 make a ¾" eye.

With color 8 do a figure-eight wrap on 2 arms by wrapping over arm 1, under and around arm 2 with 2 turns, under and around arm 1 with 2 turns until you have made 4 complete patterns. Repeat this figure-eight wrap on arms 3 and 4.

With color 3, back wrap 7 rounds. With color 2 back wrap 7 rounds. With color 4 top wrap 7 rounds.

FLAG 5:
The Mexican flag. In 1821, Texas had become part of the Empire of Mexico. The Mexican flag at that time had three vertical stripes, green on the left, white in the center and red on the right. At first the Mexican eagle was in the center of the white stripe. In 1824 the eagle was deleted and the date 1824 substituted. Texas remained under this flag until 1836 when Sam Houston defeated the Mexicans in the Battle of San Jacinto and Texas became an independent Republic.

Glue the 6" stick at the 11¼" notch.
With color 8 make a ¾" eye.

With color 7 top wrap for 4 rounds. Change to back wrap and do 5 rounds.

Taking two turns around each arm, with color 9 top wrap for 5 rounds. Taking one turn around each arm, do 1 round.

Taking two turns around each arm, with color 4 top wrap for 2 rounds. Taking one turn around each arm, do 1 round.

With color 8 top wrap for 6 rounds.

FLAG 6:
The United States flag. Texas became the 28th U.S. state on December 29, 1845. At this time the flag had 27 stars. Stars were added to the U.S. flag annually on July 4th, so the 28th star for Texas was not added until July 4, 1846. After the Civil War Texas was admitted to the Union again in 1870.

Glue the last 8" stick at the 5½" notch.
With color 2 do a ¾" eye.

Taking two turns around arm 3 and one turn on arms 1, 2, and 4, do 6 rounds of color 7.

Taking three turns around arm 3 and two turns on arms 1, 2 and 4, do 7 rounds of color 4. Do 7 rounds of color 12.

Finish by screwing the white STAR on the first flag by screwing a small wood screw from back side being careful it does not come through the STAR center. Space arms evenly to bisect eye. Trim with a fancy sequin in center.

COLORS:
1. White mohair
2. Medium blue
3. White Pliana
4. Red
5. Gold Bucilla brocade
6. Warm gold
7. White Wintuk
8. Emerald green
9. Ross (Scotch plaid) Redheart
10. Light blue
11. Bright yellow
12. Variegated red/white/blue mohair

HOPI KACHINA

Part 1

To the Hopis, an Indian tribe in Northern Arizona, the spirits in their religion are represented in carved, painted and feather-trimmed wood dolls. This ojo represents Tawa, the sun-god Kachina. Done in traditional earth colors, this ojo is typical of Indian art forms.

The ojo is done in two parts, part 1 being completed befor attaching part 2. This is done for ease of handling.

STICKS:
Cut one 26" and two 20" sticks in wide width.

GLUING:
The sticks are not notched but the 26" stick is marked in the center and the two 20" sticks marked 13" in from one end. Drill through the marks making a hole large enough to accommodate a ⅛" carriage bolt, 2½" long. Working from diagram below, put glue between the sticks at the hole. Place together with the 26" stick on the bottom and the other two sticks crossed on top. Using a template, arrange the sticks on a 40° angle to the center bottom stick. Fasten securely with the carriage bolt running up nut snugly on back, but do not cut excess off. Paint sticks chocolate brown.

PROCEDURE:
With color 1 on arm 1 and wrapping every arm make an oblong eye of 2". (See HOW TO MEASURE).

With color 2, top wrap for 4 rounds.
With color 3, back wrap for 7 rounds.
With color 4, back wrap for 4 rounds. Do not cut off.

Changing to top wrap, do 5 rounds.
With color 5 do 4 rounds.
With color 3 do 3 rounds.
With color 2 do 3 rounds.
With color 1 do 4 rounds.
With color 4 do 4 rounds.
With color 3 do 5 rounds.
With color 5 do 4 rounds.

Taking two turns around each arm:
With color 2 do 4 rounds.
With color 4 do 4 rounds.

Taking one turn around each arm, with color 1 do 3 rounds.

HEAD

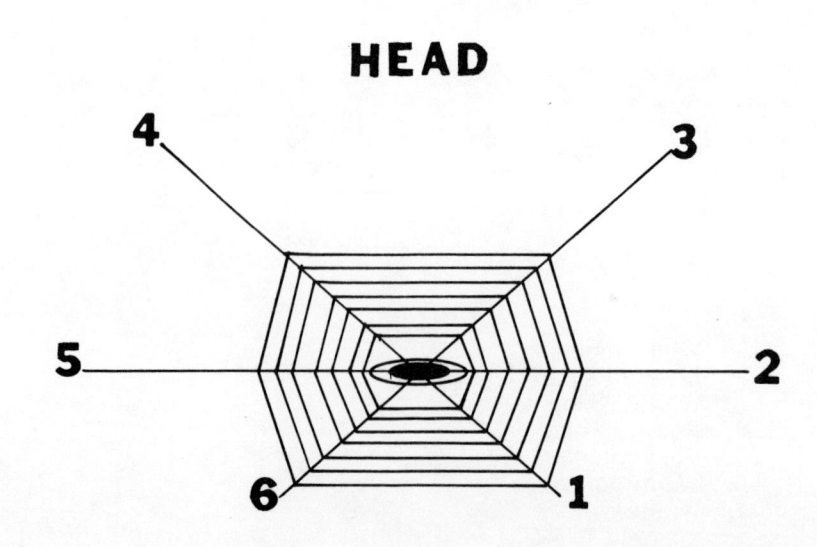

HOPI KACHINA
Part 2

STICKS:
Cut two 24" sticks in narrow width.
Cut one 8½", one 27", and three 48" sticks in wide width.

ASSEMBLY:
Mark the three 48" sticks 13" down from top end. Drill at marks to fit carriage bolt of Part 1. Paint sticks chocolate brown.

Remove carriage bolt nut from Part 1, insert end of bolt through the three 48" sticks and replace nut. Before tightening completely, attach other pieces as follows: Mark center leg (B on diagram) 8½" down from carriage bolt. Drill hole for ⅛" brass screw at mark. Mark 8½" stick in center and drill. Fasten together with screw laying the short piece (G on diagram) on top of B.

Bringing legs A and C on top of G, fasten each end with a small brass screw and carefully saw off G so angle is the same as legs A and C.

Using the 27" stick (H on diagram), fasten the center to leg B in the same manner, laying on top at 7" from bottom of B. Laying H under legs A and C, fasten ends with screw and saw off excess.

Place the two 24" narrow sticks so top is even with G and on back of both G and H. Fasten top at 2" from center screw of G. Fasten bottom at 6½" from center screw of H. Paint all exposed sticks chocolate brown.

Check carefully with diagram below and tighten carriage bolt securely.

SKIRT:
Extend wrap cross pieces G and H between legs A and C with color 1, using X crossings at screw points.

PATTERN A:
Over and around arm A
Under and around arm E
Under and around arm B
Under and around arm F
Over and around arm C, with 2 turns
Over and around arm F
Under and around arm B
Under and around arm E
Under and around arm A, with 2 turns

PATTERN B:
Over and around arm A
Passing over the top of arm E go over and around arm B
Passing over the top of arm F go over and around arm C, with 2 turns.
Passing over arm F, go under and around arm B.
Passing over arm E, go under and around arm A, with 2 turns.

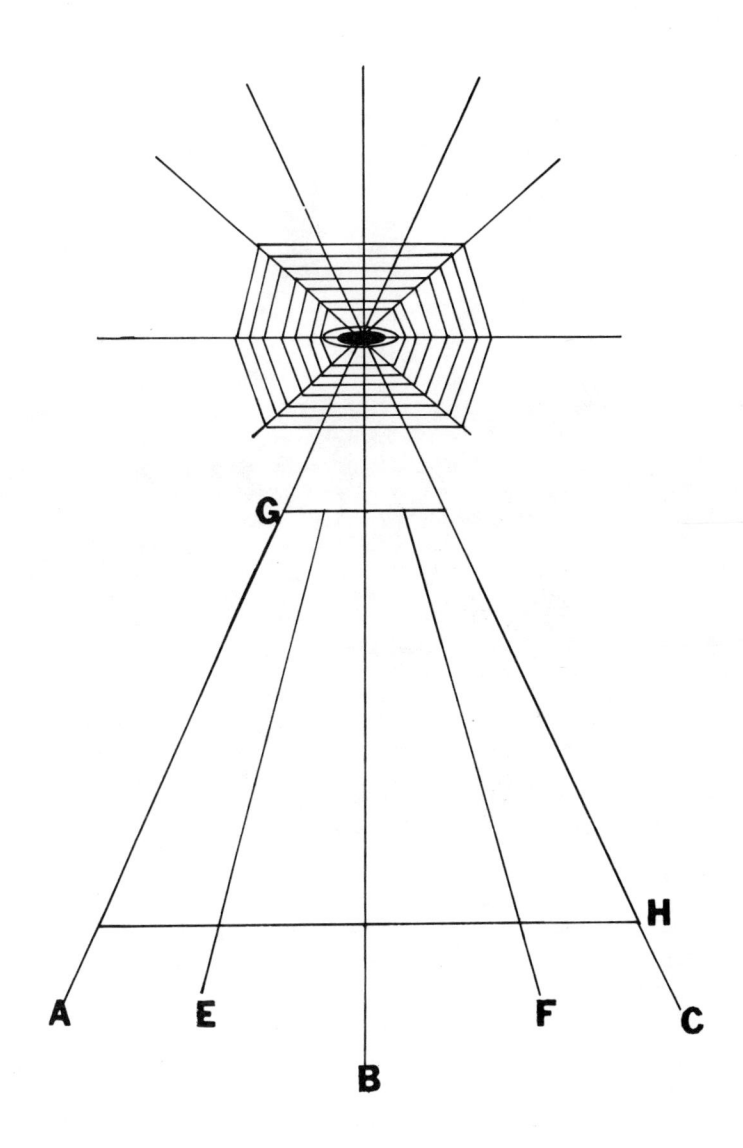

PATTERN C:
Over and around arm A
Over and around arm E
Over and around arm B
Over and around arm F
Over and around arm C, with 2 turns.
Over and around arm F
Over and around arm B
Over and around arm E
Under and around arm A, with 2 turns.

HOPI KACHINA (Cont.)

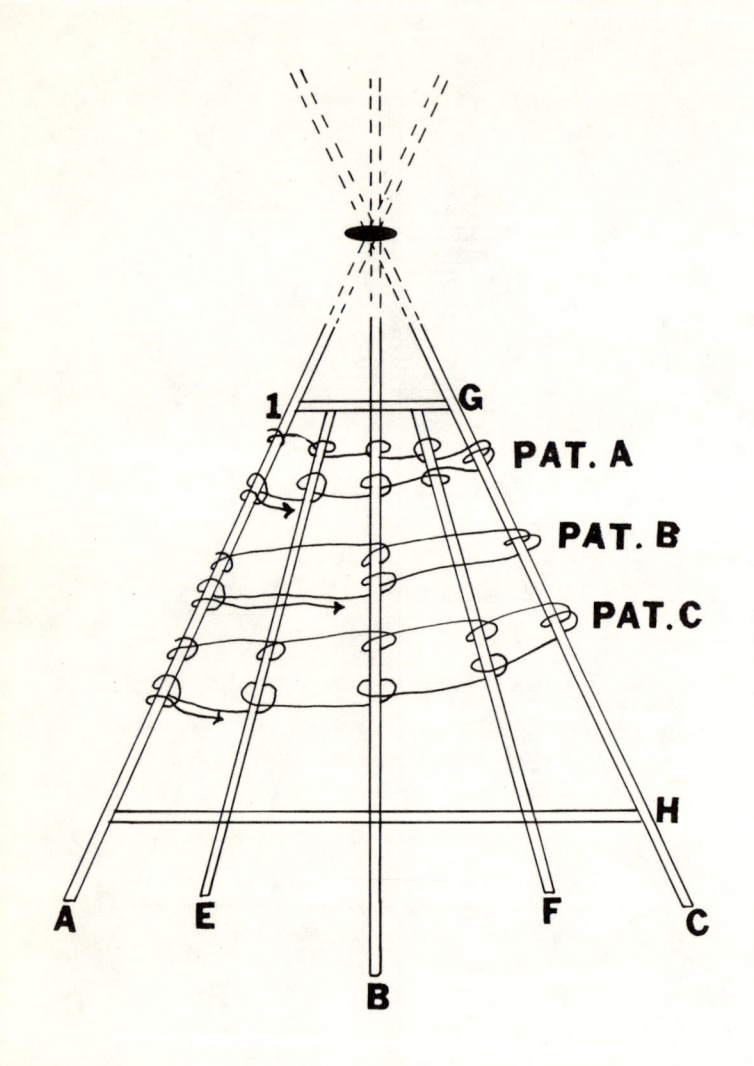

Attach color 3 at point 1 on arm A in diagram. Work pattern A for 3 patterns.

With color 2, work pattern B for 5 patterns.
With color 4, work pattern B for 7 patterns.
With color 6, work pattern B for 5 patterns.
With color 7, work pattern B for 4 patterns.

With color 3, work pattern A for 6 patterns.

With color 4, work pattern B for 4 patterns.
With color 7, work pattern B for 3 patterns.
With color 1, work pattern B for 2 patterns.
With color 2, work pattern B for 3 patterns.
With color 5, work pattern B for 5 patterns.

With color 3, work pattern A for 5 patterns.

With color 6, work pattern C for 3 patterns.
With color 7, work pattern C for 3 patterns.

Taking 3 turns around arms A and C from now to end:
With color 4, work pattern C for 4 patterns.
With color 1, work pattern C for 3 patterns.

With color 3, work pattern A for 5 patterns.

With color 2, work pattern C for 4 patterns.
With color 4, work pattern C for 3 patterns.

With color 5, work pattern B for 6 patterns.
With color 6, work pattern B for 6 patterns.
With color 7, work pattern B for 5 patterns.
With color 4, work pattern B for 5 patterns.

With color 3, work pattern A for 5 patterns or until winding on arm B meets cross stick H.

FINISHING:
Using eagle type long feathers, fasten one to arms 1, 2, 3, 4, 5, 6, and legs A, B and C under head as shown in picture. These may be stapled in place if the spine is broken by crushing with a pair of pliers before stapling. Then the staple may be concealed under a fluff feather glued in place.

Hang by attaching a sawtooth hanger lengthwise on top of stick B. See HELPFUL HINTS.

COLORS:
1. Reynolds Vendome (an acrylic tweed of cream/brown/rust)
2. Burnt orange
3. Fisherman cream
4. Wood brown
5. Burnt orange Madison
6. Fruit of the Loom Navajo
7. Golden tan

CALIFORNIA CATAMARAN

A catamaran is a two-hulled sailing vessel originally used by Polynesian people. It is believed the Hawaiians crossed the Pacific from Tahiti on catamarans.

STICKS:
Cut one 32", two 19", and two 22" sticks wide width.

NOTCHING:
Notch the 32" stick 7¾" from each end. Notch 22" sticks 14½" up. Do not notch the 19" sticks.

GLUING:
Glue a 22" stick for left ojo at notch on the 32" stick following diagram below. It will be easier if you work the left ojo before gluing the second stick to make the right ojo. Paint sticks deep rose.

PROCEDURE:
LEFT OJO:

Attach color 1 on arm 1 and do a 1¾" eye.

Attach color 2 on arm 1 and beginning vertical diamond wrap (See TERMINOLOGY) with 2 turns around arms 1 and 3 and 1 turn around arms 2 and 4, do 16 rounds. Using same wrap outline with 2 rounds of color 1.

Attach color 3 on arm 1 and begin horizontal diamond wrap (See TERMINOLOGY) by taking 2 turns on arms 2 and 4 and 1 turn on arms 1 and 3. Do 8 rounds.

Returning to vertical diamond wrap with color 2 on arm 1 do 11 rounds, taking 1 turn around arms 2, 3 and 4 and 2 turns around arm 1.

Attach color 3 on arm 1. Taking 2 turns on arms 1, 2, and 4, and 1 turn on arm 3, do 7 rounds. Now changing to 3 turns on arm 1, 2 turns on arms 2 and 4 and 1 turn on arm 3, do 11 rounds. (The yarn on arm 2 should be 14½" in from left end of the 32" stick.) Without gluing off extend wrap arm 1 to bottom.

Glue the remaining 22" stick at right ojo notch.

RIGHT OJO:
With color 1 do a 1¾" eye. With color 2, do a horizontal diamond wrap taking 2 turns around arms 2A and 4A and 1 turn around arms 1A and 3A. In same wrap outline with 2 rounds of color 1.

Attach color 3 on arm 1A. Taking 2 turns around each arm, do 9 rounds.

Attach color 2 on arm 1A. Taking 1 turn around arms 1A, 2A, and 3A and 2 turns around arm 4A, do 11 rounds. Attach color 3 on arm 3A. Taking 1 turn around arms 4A, 1A, and 2A and 3 turns around arm 3A, do 22 rounds. Without gluing off, extend wrap arm 3A to end. (Cover any unwrapped stick between the two ojos by extend wrapping with color 3.)

FINISHING:
Make four large (2¾") pompons using all three colors and attach firmly to arms 1, 1A, 3 and 3A. Make two 7" French tassels (See MAKING ENDS NEAT) and attach to arms 2A and 4A.

Extend wrap both 19" sticks using all three colors.

Fasten 19" sticks to arms 1 and 1A and 3 and 3A with wood screws, from back side, trimming stick ends so they do not extend beyond pompons.

Hang with a loop on arm 3 and also arm 3A.

COLORS:
1. Raspberry
2. Light pink
3. Medium rose

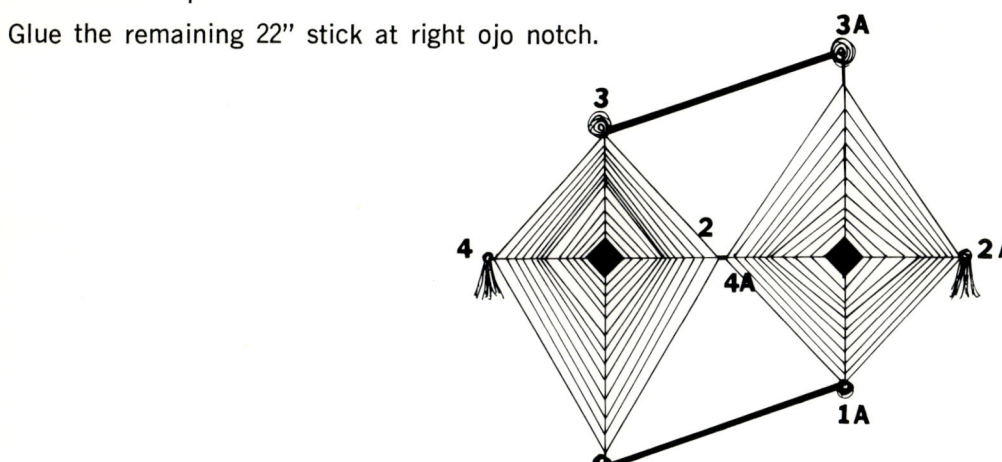

25

CALIFORNIA CATAMARAN

GRANDMOTHER'S FAN

PARTY TIME

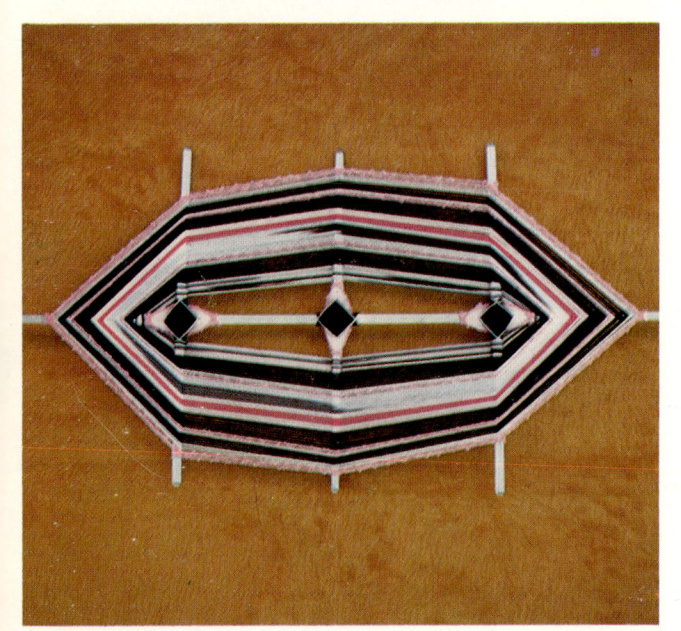

CONCHA

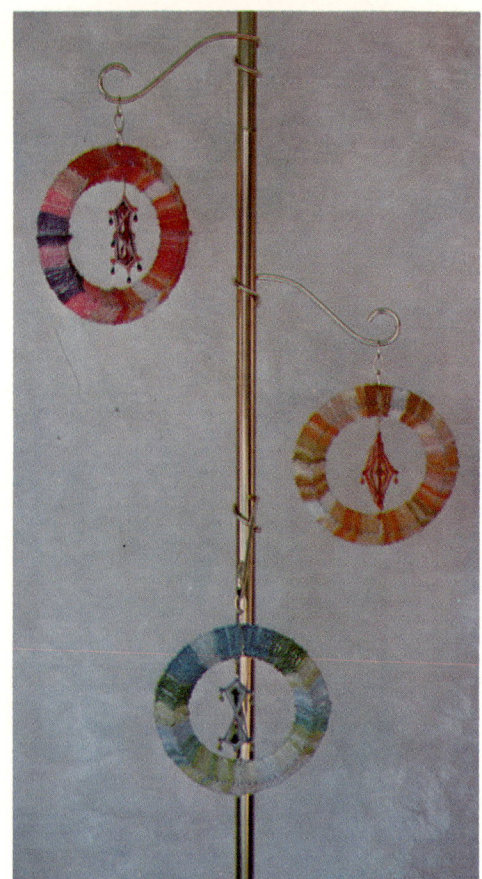

PLANTER POLE

KANEHOE

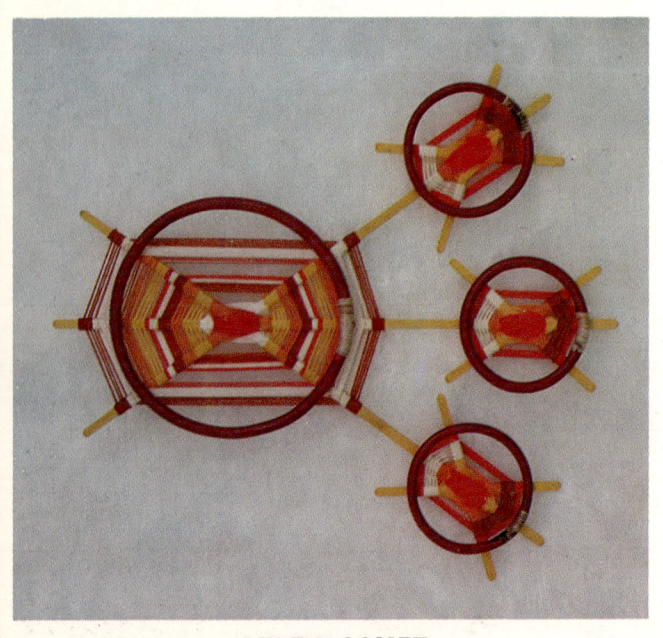

PELE'S COMET

TANNENBAUM

HOPI KACHINA	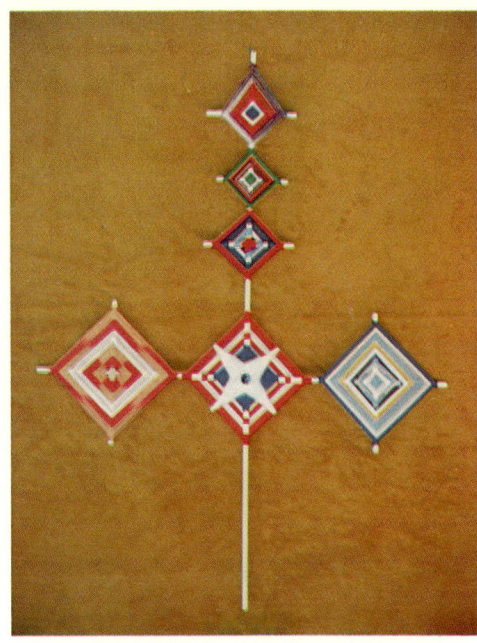 SIX FLAGS OVER TEXAS	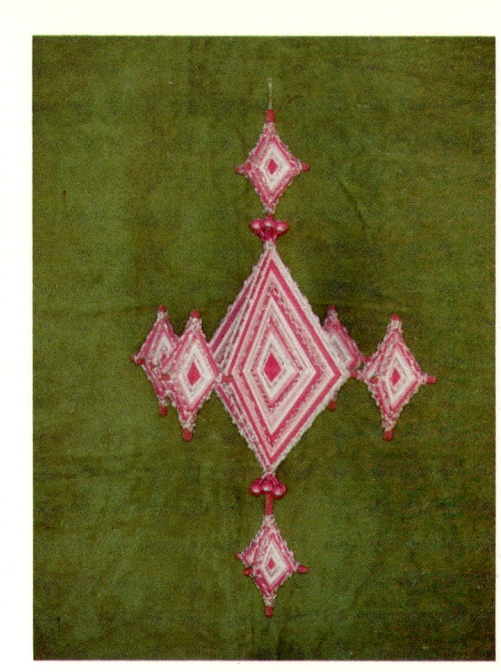 TITANIA
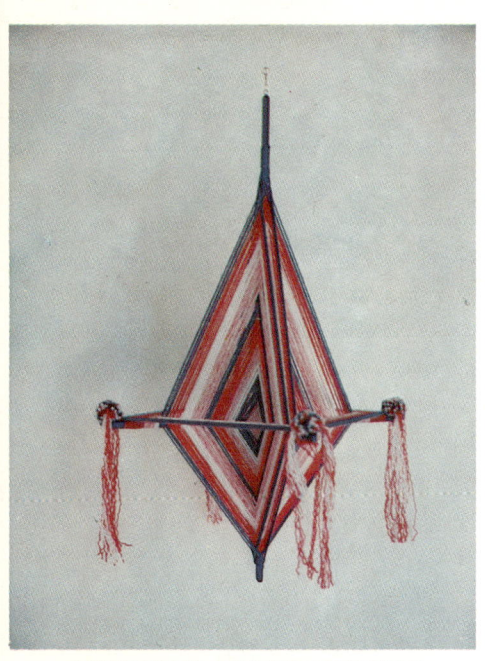 AMERICAN SPACE SHUTTLE	 FIJI FAN	 NAVAHO BRAVE
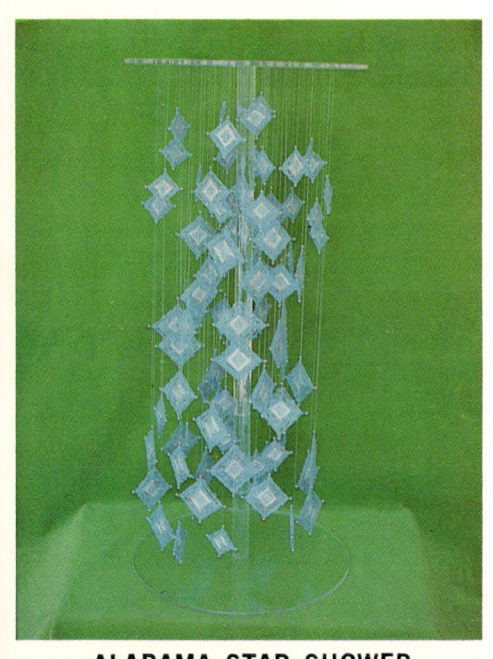 ALABAMA STAR SHOWER	 FIESTA TIME IN JUAREZ	 CHRISTMAS IN ARIZONA

SEMINOLE

The pattern on this ojo is copied from the lovely patchwork skirts worn by the Seminole women.

STICKS:
Cut four 18" sticks in narrow width.

NOTCHING:
Notch all sticks in center; bevel ends.

GLUING:
Glue sticks together to make two basic ojos, then fasten into a shield shape with a small brass screw through the centers and secure with a nut. Paint arms 6 and 8 white, other arms dark blue.

PROCEDURE:
Attach color 1 back of arm 1. Cross between arms 6 and 3 to between arms 1 and 5, cross between arms 3 and 7 to between arms 8 and 1. Repeat four times to cover center.

Continuing with color 1, make a flower eye (See TERMINOLOGY) measuring ¾" from the center and gluing off on arm 5.

Wrapping every arm in sequence;
With color 2 on arm 1, do 3 rounds.
With color 3 on arm 1, do 2 rounds.
With color 4 on arm 1, do 2 rounds.
With color 1 on arm 1, do 3 rounds.

With color 2 on arm 8, do 3 rounds; without gluing off extend wrap to within ½" of arm end. Attach color 2 on arm 6 and extend wrap to within ½" of arm end.

Attach color 4 on arm 1. Triple figure-eight wrap (See TERMINOLOGY) for four patterns. Attach color 5 on arm 1 and do seven patterns. Attach color 1 on arm 1 and do five patterns. Attach color 2 on arm 1 and do fourteen patterns. Attach color 3 on arm 1 and do six patterns.

Attach color 4 on arm 1 and do four patterns. Attach color 1 on arm 1 and do three patterns. With color 2, do six patterns.

Using the same color sequence work a triple figure-eight wrap on arms 3, 7, and 4, to match.

FINISHING:
Finish each arm with a plastic teardrop jewel obtainable in craft shops, used for making fancy lamps.

Hang this ojo from arm 3 (when hung from arm 6 this could be a variation of La Mariposa appearing in the Creative Ojo Book.)

COLORS:
1. Dark blue
2. White Wintuk Pompadour baby yarn
3. Blue tweed
4. Light blue
5. Medium blue

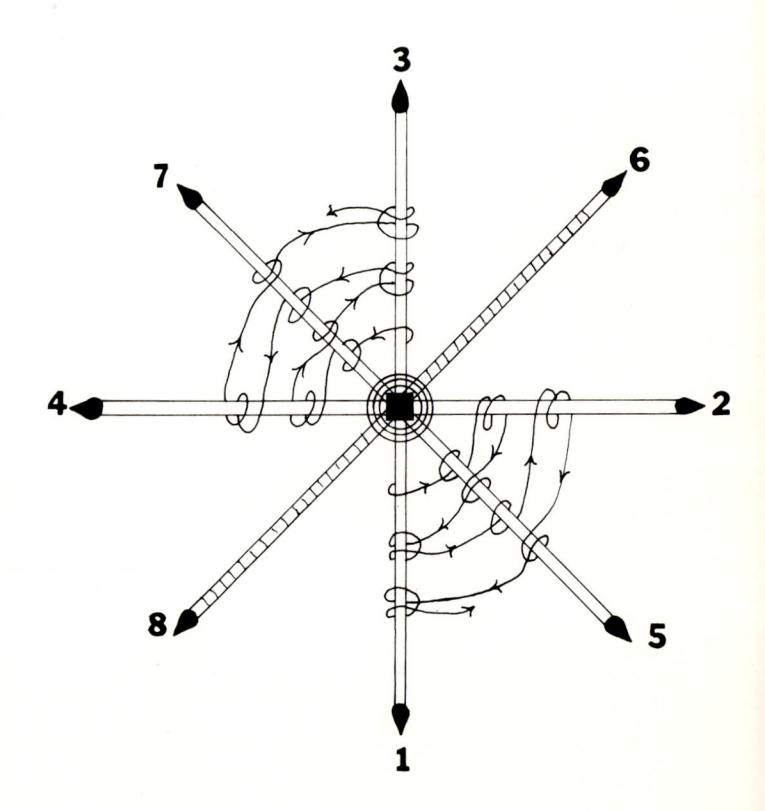

SARASOTA SPIRAL

The frame for this ojo was made of welding rod, welded in center and shaped as shown in diagram. It may also be made of heavy coat hanger wire, either welded together or glued with an adhesive such as Epoxy. Enlarge the diagram below fitting it into a 16" circle.

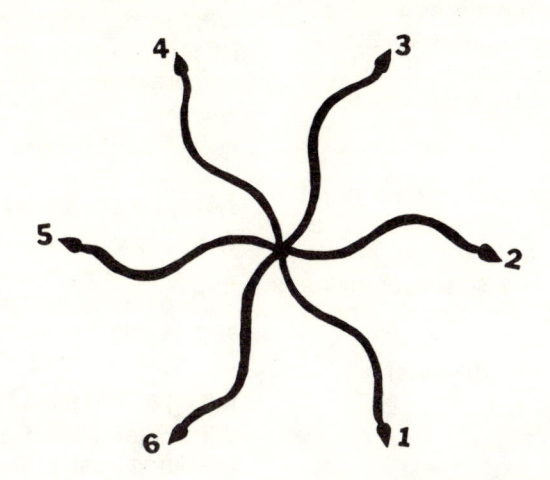

PROCEDURE:
PATTERN:
PART A: Using a figure 8 wrap, go over and around arm 1, under and around arm 2, over and around arm 3 taking 2 turns, over and around arm 2, under and around arm 1 taking 2 turns.

PART B: Using a figure 8 wrap, go over and around arm 4, under and around arm 5, over and around arm 6 taking 2 turns, over and around arm 5, under and around arm 4 taking 2 turns.

With color 1 and working PART A pattern, do 7 rounds. With color 2 do 6 rounds.

String ten ¼" magenta glass beads (packed 50 in a bag) on color 3. Using PART A pattern wind, place 5 beads between arms 1 and 2, and 5 beads between arms 2 and 3. Glue off on arm 3.
With color 4 do 2 rounds.
With color 5 do 5 rounds.
With color 3 do 6 rounds.
With color 1 do 7 rounds.
String 26 beads on color 3 and work in pattern using 13 beads between arms 1 and 2, and arms 2 and 3.
With color 2 do 10 rounds.
With color 4 do 4 rounds.

Taking an extra turn around arms 1 and 3, follow PART A pattern with 6 rounds of color 5.
Returning to 2 turns around arms 1 and 3, do 2 rounds of color 4.

Using the same sequence of colors and beadwork, do PART B pattern on arms 4, 5, 6.

FINISHING:
Fasten six magenta tear-drop pendants, used in lamp shade making, on spiral arms with either Epoxy glue or "Stickum", available in florist supply shops.
Hang by arm 4.

VARIATION:
This ojo may be hung as a mobile, since both sides are wound alike, by attaching a medium size fishing swivel to a nylon hanging thread. In this case two pendant jewels should be used on each arm, gluing together back to back.

COLORS:
1. Royal blue Madison
2. Light blue Madison
3. White Madison
4. Unger #9 in blue/green/yellow
5. Red purple Sparkle

ALABAMA STAR SHOWER

This modern ojo may be adapted to any size or height desired. It could even be used as a mobile by eliminating the base and supporting rod. Placed with a light behind it the plastic becomes a living rainbow. Instead of a monotone, multi-colored ojos may be substituted.

SUPPLIES:
You will need 352 light blue pearlhead pins, either round or oval, 2" long. Material required is one tube of silver elastic yarn (50 yards), two kinds of bouclé yarn, preferably one silk and one cotton, and two spools of nylon crystal sewing thread in clear color. You will also need two circles of Plexiglas, 14" in diameter, ¼" thick and one solid Plexiglas rod 36" long, 1" in diameter.

PROCEDURE:
Either solder or epoxy pins together as follows:
Make 32 large ojos (3¼" long) by fastening pins together as close to the points as possible. You will have a basic mini ojo with the pearl heads forming the ends of your working sticks. Make 40 small (2¼") ojos by bringing the points close to the pearl heads. Make 16 medium (2¾") ojos by bringing points halfway back on pin. Be sure ojo frames are square.

Small Mini Ojos:
With color 1 do a double eye of 3 rounds (See TERMINOLOGY). With color 2, wrapping first one side and then the other do 3 rounds. With color 3, wrapping first one side and then the other and taking 2 turns around each arm, do 3 rounds.

Medium Mini Ojos:
With color 1 do a double eye of 3 rounds. With color 2 wrapping first one side and then the other, do 3 rounds. With color 3, wrapping first one side and then the other and taking 2 turns around each arm, do 4 rounds.

Large Mini Ojos:
With color 1 do a double eye of 4 rounds. With color 2 wrapping first one side and then the other do 4 rounds. With color 3 wrapping first one side and then the other and taking 2 turns around each arm, do 5 rounds.

HINTS:
You will find it easier when working on the pins to double half hitch your ends rather than glue them. Be sure to pull snugly to avoid riding down the arm. A line of glue when applying color 3 will help hold yarn in place.

You may use toothpicks for the small and medium ojos instead of the pearlhead pins and trim with small beads glued on the toothpick ends, but in making the large size, you will have to substitute barbeque sticks for the toothpicks.

COLORS
1. Light blue silk bouclé
2. Silver elastic yarn (50 yard tube)
3. Light blue cotton bouclé

ALABAMA STAR SHOWER (Cont.)

Using the Plexiglas circle as a pattern, make a paper circle the same size. Fold the paper circle in half, then half again until you have four folds. (Wide edge will be about 2¾") Opening the paper pattern and using a compass, draw circles 1¼", 2½", 3¾" and 5" from center. Mark a dot along the creased lines where they intersect the drawn circles. Use a felt tip pen. Mark midway between the dots on the outer circle, and midway between every other dot on the 3¾" circle. You will have 16 dots on the first two circles, 24 dots on the third circle and 32 dots on the outer circle.

Lay the paper template on a wood board, lay one Plexiglas circle on top and drill 88 holes using a 1/32" drill, one hole at each dot. Be sure holes are exactly vertical. Using Plexiglas solvent, attach the rod to the center of each circle. (Instructions for using the solvent can be obtained from your plastics dealer.)

Cut 8 pieces of crystal thread 17" long and 8 pieces 22" long. Knotting the cut ends one inch down, attach 16 small ojos by running the knot through the center loop of thread and drawing up tightly on arm 3. Using a small needle, run the knotted ends up through the holes on the 1¼" circle, temporarily fastening in place with a small piece of Scotch tape.

Using the same method and 27" of thread, fasten 16 of the medium ojos in every hole of the 2½" circle.

Using 37" lengths of thread on 16 of the large ojos, fasten in the creased line holes of the 3¾" circle. With 20" pieces of thread, fasten 8 small ojos in remaining holes.

Using 46" lengths of thread on the remaining 16 large ojos, fasten in every other hole of the 5" circle. Using 14" pieces of thread, fasten the remaining 16 small ojos in the midway holes.

Working from the inner circle out, adjust one ojo at a time to different heights to make a pleasing arrangement and refasten with tape. When you have the ojos placed to suit, touch a small drop of Duco airplane cement to top of hole (be sure tape does not cover hole). Allow to dry overnight, use another drop of cement and allow to dry overnight. Carefully snip threads close to hole and remove tape.

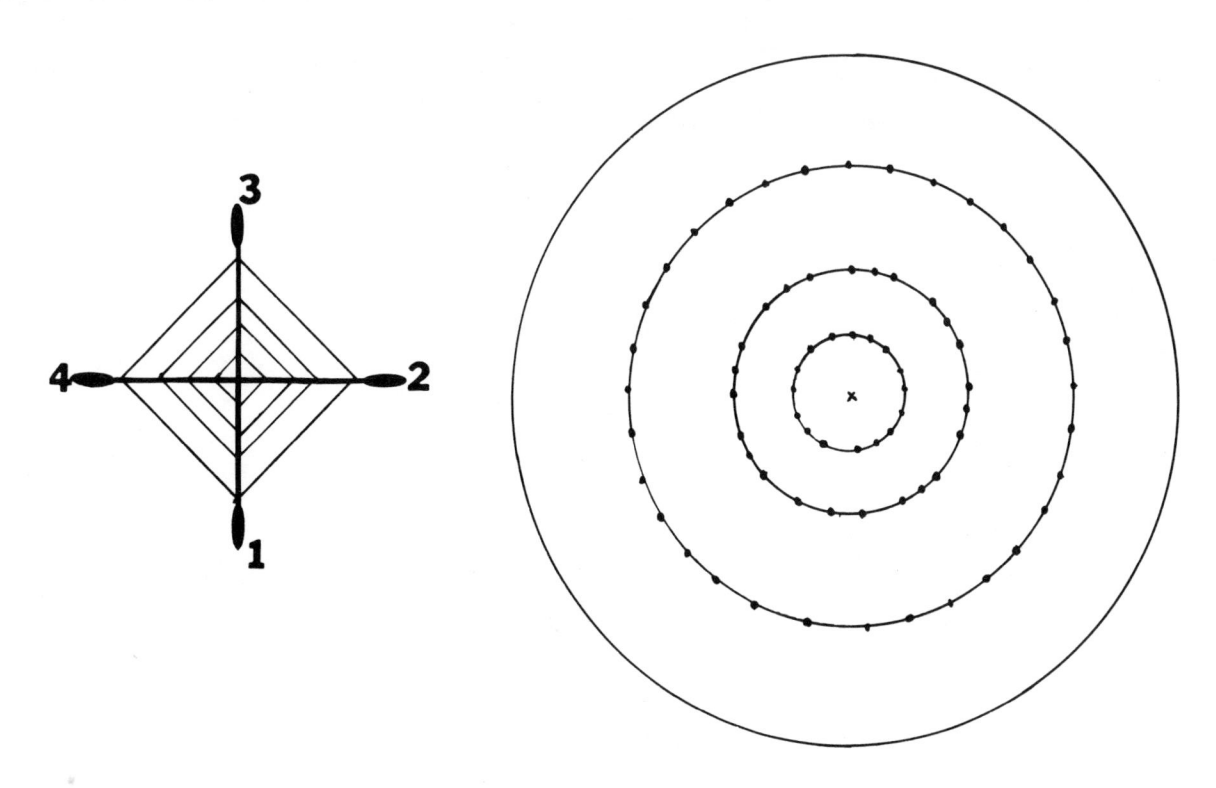

GRANDMOTHER'S QUILT

Inspired by the quilting patterns of the Kentucky mountains, this ojo is most effective when made entirely of Madison bouclé. However, it may be made of single ply Persian or tapestry yarns.

MATERIALS REQUIRED:

One inner ring of a 10" blue plastic hoop, one inner ring of a 14" yellow plastic hoop. (Hoop-De-Doos are available in knit shops, variety stores, some markets and most department stores.) Three 12" fireplace matches, with the heads cut off. Eighteen 6" bar-b-q sticks with points cut off, then cut in half.

GLUING:

Glue twelve pairs of bar-b-q sticks into twelve basic 3" ojos.

PROCEDURE:

Wind small amounts of yarn into small balls to facilitate wrapping within the hoop.

Using a template, drill both hoops every 30° with a small drill fitted to the bar-b-q sticks. Enlarge every other hole on the blue ring to fit the fireplace matches.

Insert the fireplace matches in the 60° holes of the blue ring. Dab a small amount of glue on the outside of the ring to hold the sticks in place. Allow to dry thoroughly.

INNER OJO:

With color 1 do a ½" flower eye (See TERMINOLOGY).

With color 2 do 5 rounds.
With color 3 do 7 rounds.

With color 4, star wrap (See TERMINOLOGY) for 7 rounds on arms 1, 3, 5.

With color 4, star wrap for 7 rounds on arms 2, 4, 6.

Attach colors 5 and 6 in opposite directions below each other on arm 1 for double color wrap (See TERMINOLOGY). In double color wrap do 5 rounds.

With color 7 on arm 1, Triple figure-eight wrap by going over arm 1, under and around arm 2, over and around arm 3 with 1½ turns, over and around arm 2, under and around arm 1 with 1½ turns. Do 4 complete rounds returning to arm 1. In same wrap, with color 8 do 3 complete rounds. With color 9, do 7 complete rounds.

Attach color 7 on arm 4 and working arms 4, 5, 6 do same Triple figure-eight wrap to match. With color 8 on arm 4 do 3 complete rounds. With color 9 on arm 4 do 7 complete rounds.

Attach color 10 on arm 6 and back wrap for 6 rounds.

Attach color 4 on arm 6 and back wrap for 4 rounds.

Taking two turns around each arm, with color 1 do 3 rounds. With color 2 do 4 rounds. With color 3 do 3 rounds.

Attaching colors 5 and 6 on arm 1, repeat double color wrap for 6 rounds.

With color 7 on arm 1 back wrap to the end of the sticks, about 8 rounds.

OUTER OJOS

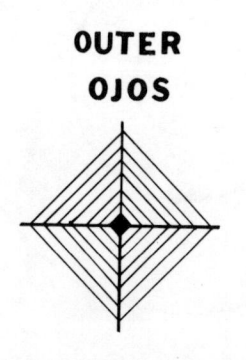

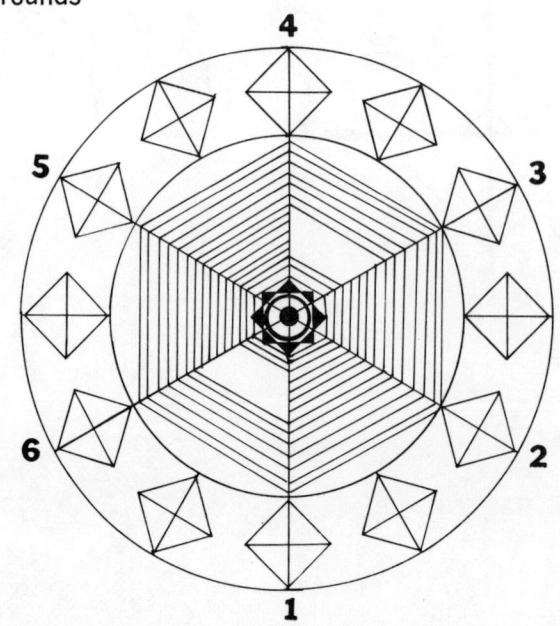

GRANDMOTHER'S QUILT (Cont.)

MINI OJOS:

Working the 3" ojo frames, make twelve mini ojos for the outer ring by doing a ¼" eye, then 3 rounds of each color, as listed below. This will only make a 1½" ojo, but you need the extra length for ease of handling.

OJO 1: Colors 9, 4, 5, 7, 3
OJO 2: Colors 1, 7, 10, 8, 9
OJO 3: Colors 3, 2, 10, 4, 7
OJO 4: Colors 5, 2, 9, 7, 1
OJO 5: Colors 10, 6, 2, 1, 4
OJO 6: Colors 7, 9, 4, 2, 5
OJO 7: Colors 5, 2, 4, 9, 7
OJO 8: Colors 4, 1, 2, 6, 10
OJO 9: Colors 1, 7, 9, 2, 5
OJO 10: Colors 7, 4, 10, 2, 3
OJO 11: Colors 9, 8, 10, 7, 1
OJO 12: Colors 3, 7, 5, 4, 9

Secure last round with glue on all 4 arms.

FINISHING:

Run twelve bar-b-q stick pieces through each one of the holes on the outer yellow ring. Fasten against the blue ring with glue where sticks meet fireplace matches.

On the alternate holes, insert sticks in holes of the blue ring and secure with glue. Trim any stick extending beyond yellow ring when dry.

With nippers cut sticks on mini ojos as close to winding as possible. Lay a line of glue along each outer stick and along the back of each mini ojo. Lay in place and allow to dry.

Attach hanger to the back of arm 5 using color 9 and going through color 9 of the figure-eight wrap.

COLORS:

1. Purple Madison bouclé
2. Pink Madison bouclé
3. Red Madison bouclé
4. Light blue Madison bouclé
5. Peacock Madison bouclé
6. Lavendar Madison bouclé
7. Yellow Madison bouclé
8. Light orange Madison bouclé
9. Dark orange Madison bouclé
10. Emerald Madison bouclé

GRANDMOTHER'S FAN

The open work design on this fan is copied from authentic fans made in America in the late 1800's. Called Peek-a-boo fans, the open space was usually backed by fine lace. The fans were used in theatres where the open work design allowed the lady to cover her face when anything in the play embarrassed her and yet miss nothing of the action on stage.

STICKS:

Four sticks, 24" long, wide width. Point both ends. Paint rich blue. One 8 x 10 gilded oval picture frame (wooden) available for around $3.00 in large chain frame shops.

ASSEMBLY:

Drill a hole 1" up on each stick, centering it, the size to accommodate a bolt 1/8" or 3/16" in diameter, 2" long. Since the sticks cannot be taken apart again, at this point you must attach the tassel and any trim you wish. On the sample made and pictured, a piece of old jewelry was used for decoration, the stone in the center being removed so the bolt could be inserted. Fasten loosely with a nut.

Using template, arrange the sticks at the 15° and the 45° marks, placing the bolt at the center of the template circle. Secure bolt firmly with a nut.

Holding the picture frame horizontally, lay on the sticks so outside rim of frame is at 8" up from stick ends. Using four brass bolts 1½" long, fasten frame to sticks securing with nuts on back. When drilling the holes for the bolts, be sure they are vertical. Turn assembly over and carefully saw frame at outside edges of sticks 1 and 4.

PROCEDURE:

Except where noted, attach all yarn to arm 4.
With color 1, fan wrap (See TERMINOLOGY) for 4 patterns.

With color 2, fan wrap for 3 patterns.

With color 3, extend wrap (See TERMINOLOGY) for 12 rounds. Do not cut off, but carry to arm 3 and extend wrap 12 rounds. Do not cut off, but carry to arm 2, and extend wrap for 12 rounds. Do not cut off, but carry to arm 1, extend wrap for 12 rounds and glue off on arm 1.

DOING ALL FAN WRAP:

With color 4, do 6 patterns.
With color 5, do 2 patterns.
With color 6, do 4 patterns.
With color 7, do 4 patterns.
With color 2, do 2 patterns.
With color 1, do 6 patterns.
With color 5, do 3 patterns.
With color 8, do 5 patterns.

Attach color 3 on arm 1 and extend wrap arm 1 for 1¼".
Do not cut off. Carry yarn to arm 2, extend wrap for 1¼".
Do not cut off. Carry yarn to arm 3, extend wrap for 1¼".
Do not cut off. Carry yarn to arm 4, extend wrap for 1¼", and glue off on arm 4.

DOING ALL FAN WRAP:

With color 2, do 5 patterns.
With color 9, do 2 patterns.
With color 1, do 3 patterns.
With color 7, do 3 patterns.
With color 6, do 3 patterns.
With color 4, do 5 patterns.
With color 2, do 3 patterns.
With color 9, do 3 patterns.

Attach picture hangers behind arms 2 and 3.

COLORS:

1. Medium blue
2. Coral
3. Gold Bucilla brocade
4. Blue and white Sosi (a 2-ply yarn from Israel.)
5. Unger #9 in yellow/green/gold
6. Yellow
7. Blue-emerald Dazzleaire
8. Nile green
9. Unger #9 in pink/coral/lavendar

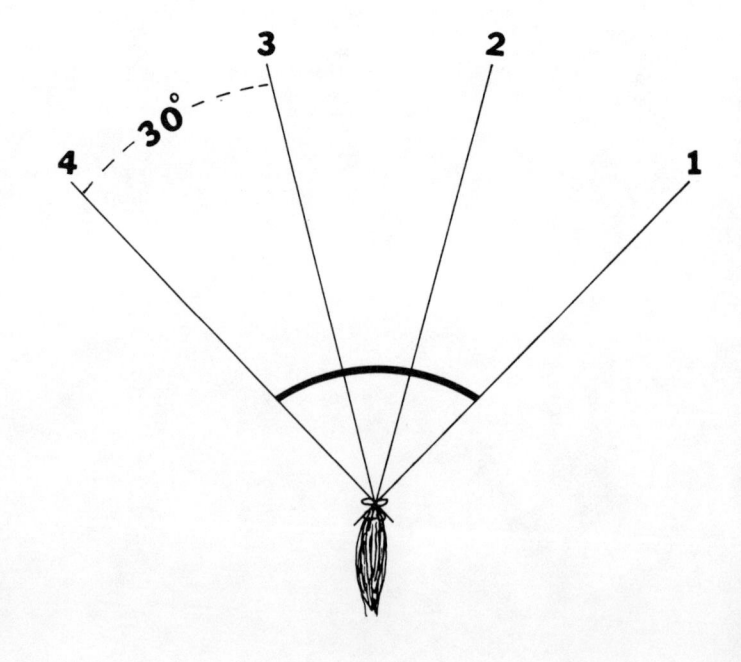

HEX-A-GON

The hex signs found on Pennsylvania Dutch barns are an important part of American folk art. Most of the barn signs were done either by the farmer or a traveling artist, who used a homemade compass which was simply a piece of rope tied to a nail with a piece of chalk on the rope's free end. Their design has been said to have derived from symbols of ancient civilizations and in the back country of Germany faded examples may still be found on old buildings. The use of geometrics with such symbols as hearts is commonly found in Pennsylvania Dutch country.

STICKS:
Cut three 14" sticks in narrow width. Do not notch.

GLUING:
Using a template lay the three sticks to make an evenly spaced pattern by putting the sticks on the 30, 60, and 90° angles. Instead of gluing, drill a small hole through the center, insert a brass screw, and secure on the back with a nut. Trim off any excess. Do not bevel ends. Paint bright yellow.

PROCEDURE:
With color 1, do a flower eye (See TERMINOLOGY) for 8 rounds.

Wing wrap pattern:
* With color 2, wing wrap arms 1 and 4 for ¾".
  With color 3, wing wrap arms 2 and 5 for ¾".
  With color 4, wing wrap arms 3 and 6 for ¾".
Repeat from * twice, making a total of 3 sets of wing wraps.
Taking 2 turns around each arm, repeat these wing wrap patterns in the same sequence and for the same distance 4 times in all. You should end up with about ½" of unwrapped arm. Also the center of the ojo will have a small unwrapped area.

FINISHING:
Using the outside ring of a 14" yellow plastic Hoop-De-Doo, available in knitting shops, place ojo so arm 3 is at the tightening screw. Carefully marking the center of arms 1, 2, 4, 5 and 6 on the outside of the ring, drill a ⅛" hole and insert a ⅛" screw, non tapered, **do not tighten excessively or you will crack plastic ring.** It will be necessary to pull ring out of round to fasten arms. This will not be noticed when ojo is hung.

COLORS:
1. Bright yellow
2. Coffee brown
3. Watermelon Wintuk
4. Turquoise Wintuk

Chenille Cone Heart Symbols

Measure carefully and mark the center point between each pair of arms on the outside of the plastic ring. Drill a small hole large enough to accommodate the size bar-b-q sticks you will use to hold the hearts in place. These sticks can be bought at any gourmet or Oriental shop. Sticks should slide easily into the hole, yet be tight enough not to drop out.

Using the pattern below, cut six hearts from ½" thick styrofoam. You may be able to find pre-cut hearts at a florist supply house. They will be more attractive if painted red. Be sure to obtain paint for styrofoam, available in spray cans at hobby shops.

Using approximately 50 twelve-inch chenille stems in bright yellow, available in craft shops, cut in half. Make chenille "buttons" by using a cone chenille curler. You may buy the tool in a craft shop or you may make your own by inserting 2 small nails in a ½" diameter dowel stick, cutting the heads off the nails.

To curl the chenille, place the end of a chenille stem between the nails allowing ½" to stick out at the right. Bend this piece down. Turning the wood dowel in your hand curling the chenille around the stick. Remove from slotted end, press down to partially flatten the cone, and insert beginning stem in styrofoam heart. Cover the hearts completely on one side, gluing in place.

Run the bar-b-q sticks, pointed end toward the center of the ojo, through the holes in the plastic ring. Using glue at indentation of heart, press heart on to the stick until it fits snugly against the inside of the ring.

Trim center by curling one 12" piece of chenille into a large cone and gluing in place.

Replace the tightening screw of the hoop with a piece of drapery chain link. Fit two more pieces together and attach to the first link for hanging.

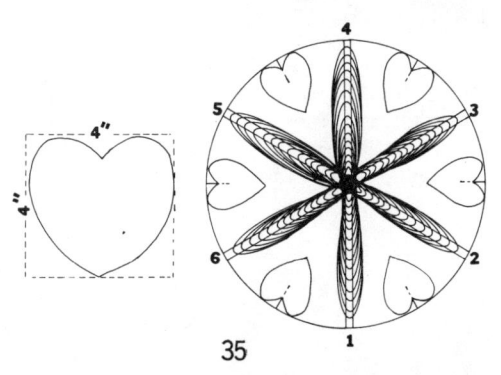

BARN OWL

The ojo design in barn owl is an adaptation of a Pennsylvania barn protective sign (often called a hex sign) and the owl is typical of farming country as it is made of corn husks. Originally intended to protect the farm household from witches, the barn signs were also placed to inform travelers the householders spoke German.

STICKS:
Cut three 24" sticks in narrow width.

NOTCHING:
Notch each stick in center. Bevel ends. Paint bright green.

GLUING:
Using template, glue the three sticks together on 30° angles. Let dry thoroughly.

PROCEDURE:
STAR WRAP PATTERN A:
Go under arm 2, over and around arm 3, under arm 4, over and around arm 5, under arm 6, over and around arm 1.

STAR WRAP PATTERN B:
Go under arm 3, over and around arm 4, under arm 5, over and around arm 6, under arm 1, over and around arm 2.

Attach color 1 on arm 1 and do 1¼" eye, wrapping every arm. Do not glue off but start **STAR WRAP PATTERN A**. Do ½" measured along arm 1. With color 1 on arm 2 do **STAR WRAP PATTERN B** for ½" measured along arm 2.

With color 2 on arm 1 repeat pattern A for 8 rounds.
With color 2 on arm 2 repeat pattern B for 8 rounds.
Attach color 3 on arm 1 and top wrap every arm for 2 rounds.
Attach color 4 on arm 1 and top wrap every arm for 4 rounds.
Attach color 3 on arm 1 and top wrap every arm for 2 rounds.
Attach color 4 on arm 1 and top wrap every arm for 6 rounds.
Attach color 3 on arm 1 and top wrap every arm for 2 rounds.
Attach color 5 on arm 1 and repeat PATTERN A for 9 rounds.
Attach color 5 on arm 2 and repeat PATTERN B for 9 rounds.

Attach color 1 on arm 1. Working on each arm, back wrap for 5 rounds. With color 2 on arm 1, back wrap for 3 rounds. With color 3 on arm 1, back wrap for 2 rounds. **Taking 2 turns around each arm,** attach color 4 on arm 1 and back wrap for 4 rounds. With color 3 on arm 1, back wrap for 2 rounds.

Taking 2 turns around each arm, attach color 5 on arm 1 and wing wrap for 7 rounds on arms 1 and 4. Attach color 5 on arm 2 and wing wrap for 7 rounds on arms 2 and 5. Attach color 5 on arm 3 and wing wrap for 7 rounds on arms 3 and 6.
Attach color 1 on arm 1. **Taking 2 turns around arms,** repeat **Pattern A** for 15 rounds. Attach color 1 on arm 5 and repeat **Pattern B** for 15 rounds. Attach color 2 on arm 1 and repeat **Pattern A** for 7 rounds. Attach color 2 on arm 2 and repeat **Pattern B** for 7 rounds.
Attach color 5 on arm 1. **Taking 3 turns,** wing wrap arms 1 and 3 for 5 rounds. Attach color 5 on arm 2, and wing wrap arms 2 and 5 for 5 rounds. Attach color 5 on arm 3 and wing wrap arms 3 and 6 for 5 rounds.

Taking only 1 turn around each arm, do 2 rounds of color 3, 4 rounds of color 4, and finish with 2 rounds of color 3.

FINISHING:
Glue small black button in center.
Attach hanger on arm 4 and fasten Corn Husk Barn Owl to arm 3 with epoxy. Because the Corn Husk Owl will tend to overbalance the ojo, it will be necessary to add a counterweight. (See COUNTERWEIGHTS under HELPFUL HINTS).

COLORS:
1. Lime green
2. Bright green
3. Black
4. Bright yellow
5. Bright red

CORN HUSK BARN OWL

Corn husks may either be obtained by peeling away the outer leaves of corn and drying in the sun until a pale cream color, or packages of the husks are available in craft and hobby shops. SELECT HUSKS THAT ARE LARGE ENOUGH TO COVER THE OWL BODY WITH ONE PIECE.

You will need a piece of foam such as is used in upholstery work, 1" thick, 6" long and 3" wide. This foam may be bought in any shop featuring upholstery materials, or you may collect scraps from an upholsterer.

Using the pattern given, cut a 2" circle for the head. The body tapers from 2½" at the bottom to 2" at the neck and is 3½" high.

Hint: Cutting foam is extremely easy if you will first saturate it with water and place in your freezer for 3 to 4 hours. It may then be cut with any sharp knife. Thaw and squeeze well.

Corn husks must be soaked to be worked. Lay the husks in a long shallow pan and pour a small amount of glycerine (obtainable in food or drug stores) over the husks, about 2 to 3 tbs. Fill the pan with hot water and allow husks to soak for at least 10 minutes.

Choosing the largest husk, at least 6" by 8" for the body, wrap carefully over the foam pattern and fasten in back with small round headed craft pins. Using fine florist wire, tie husk snugly under body at bottom. Carefully separating the bunched husk into two pieces, tie each separately ⅛" down to make feet.

Form a piece of husk at least 4" by 6" around head form and gather under neck, fastening with florist wire. Fold back any excess at sides and fasten at back of head with pins.

Using two pieces of husk 3" by 8", fold each one over 5" from bottom. Place each folded husk at neck of owl, arrange in wing-like shape down sides of body and pin in place at neck. You may have to pin the shorter piece to the body ⅓ of the way down.

When entire assembly is thoroughly dry (at least 24 hours), sketch feathers on body as shown and outline the typical heart-shaped barn owl face with a brown felt tipped pen. Glue two small black buttons on head for eyes. Glue head at top of body, reinforcing with a tooth pick if necessary. Be sure to conceal all pins, adding small bits of husk if needed.

HEX - A - GRAM

Many of the Pennsylvania barn signs use a shamrock-like design, actually a three-leaf clover, as a border trim or a center point of the sign. This version of a typical hex sign uses a six-pointed star embellished with the three-leaf clover done in chenille cones.

STICKS:
Using 6" bar-b-q sticks notch six of them 1¼" up from pointed end. Cut six 2½" sticks notching in center and sanding ends smooth.

GLUING:
Glue each small stick on the large stick to form a tree-shaped frame. Paint sticks yellow.

PROCEDURE:
The entire wrapping is done with one strand of tapestry yarn. If you use DMC yarn you may split it easily into four pieces. You will only need a three-yard piece of each color to make the star points.
The star points are made with a space tree wrap (See TERMINOLOGY) by taking 1½ turns around arms 2 and 4 and three turns around arm 3. All star points are wound the same way using the same colors.
With color 1 do 3 patterns (remember, the tree wrap is glued on on arm 2 and off on arm 4).
With color 2 do 3 patterns.
With color 3 do 4 patterns.
With color 4 do 4 patterns.
With color 5 do 3 patterns.
Wtih color 6 do 3 patterns.
With color 7 do 2 patterns.

CHENILLE CONE CLOVERS:
You will need seven styrofoam bases in clover shape, ¼" thick. These may be bought from a florist supply house or you may cut them from a sheet of plastic obtainable in your hobby store, using the pattern below. Spray yellow being sure to use styrofoam paint. Making 84 chenille cones in lime green (for instructions see HEX-A-GON), cover each clover with 12 cones placed as shown in diagram below. Glue in place.

FINISHING:
You will need one 14" plastic embroidery hoop in yellow; also one 4" wood embroidery hoop. You will use the inner ring of each hoop.
Using a template, mark the outside of the 14" hoop at the 60° marks and drill the six small holes to fit the bar-b-q sticks. Do the same with the small wooden hoop.
Insert arm 1 of each star point in the holes of the small wooden hoop, catching points where possible into one of the cone clovers which is placed in the center of the hoop. Ease arm 3 of the star points into the holes of the outside plastic hoop.
Place the six clovers between the star points, stem side against the outer hoop, and mark the hoop for holes where the stem touches.
Carefully remove star point assembly and drill small holes at clover marks on outer hoop. Reassemble the unit. Using bar-b-q sticks skewer the clovers in place. Cut excess on outside of hoop, leaving ¼" extension.
Slip a small yellow wooden bead over each stick end on the outside of the hoop and glue in place. This will keep the sticks from slipping out of the flexible hoop. Allow to dry thoroughly, then nip off any stick end which extends beyond the bead.

COLORS:
1. Orange DMC #7742
2. Emerald DMC #7943
3. Rose DMC #7603
4. Turquoise DMC #7599
5. Blue DMC #7798
6. Red DMC #7850
7. Green DMC #7912

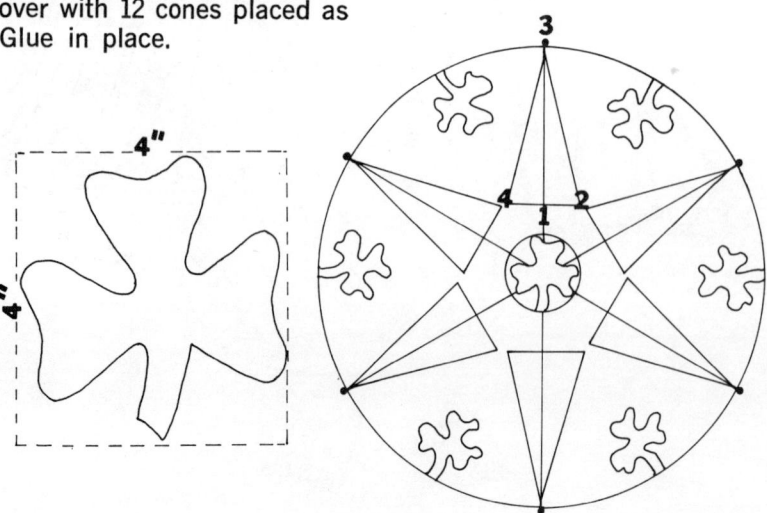

TANNENBAUM

During the American Revolution, the Hessian soldiers in America serving with the British army brought their custom of trimming a Christmas tree, a Tannenbaum, to this country. The custom had originated in Germany during the Middle Ages in the morality plays.

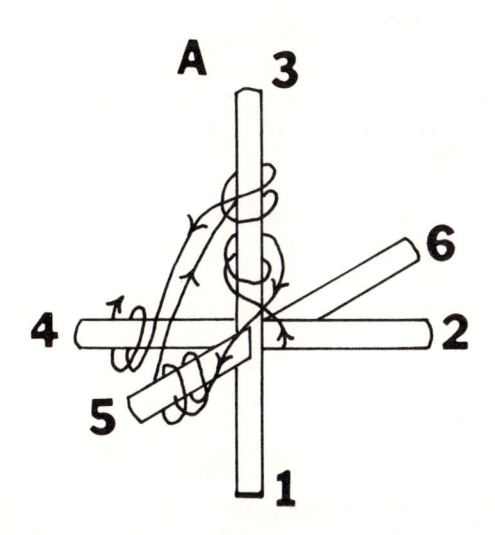

STICKS:
Cut one 16", one 18" and two 8" sticks in narrow width.

NOTCHING:
Notch the 16" stick in center and the 18" stick 3" up. Bevel ends. Bevel one end of each 8" stick.

GLUING:
Glue the 16" and 18" sticks together at notches. Cut head from 2" nail and file to point. Drill small hole through center of glued sticks and into unbeveled ends of the 8" sticks. Fill holes with glue, insert nail through ojo hole and into each end of the 8" sticks, to make a right-angled cross with the 16" ojo. Check carefully to see sticks are straight. Let dry overnight and paint bright green.

PROCEDURE:
Attach color 1 back of arm 2.
* Wrap up and over arm 3 with 1½ turns. Bring yarn down right side of arm 5 and wind two full turns coming up the left side of arm 3. Taking 1½ turns around arm 3, come down the face of arm 4. Take 2 complete turns around arm 4 coming up on back side. Give ojo a half turn to right. You are now looking at back side of arms 2 and 4 and arm 6 is pointing toward you. Going across back side of arm 3 take 1½ turns around arm 3, coming down the right side of arm 6. Take 2 full turns around arm 6 coming up the left side of arm 3 as you face the back side. Take 1½ turns around arm 3, come across the back side of arm 2, taking two full turns around arm 2. Repeat from *.

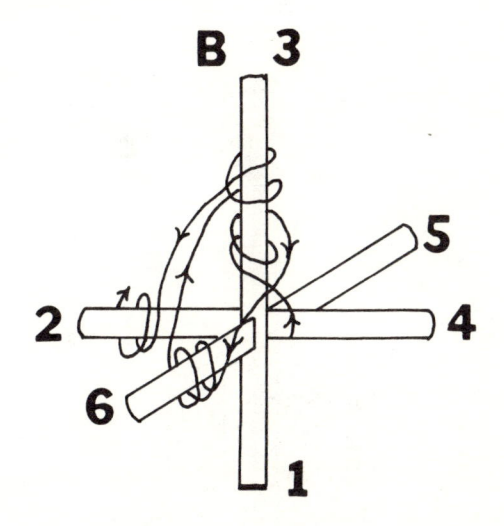

Following this pattern of wrapping, work as follows:
Do 4 rounds of color 1.
Do 2 rounds of color 2.
Do 2 rounds of color 3.
Do 4 rounds of color 4.
Do 2 rounds of color 5.
Do 3 rounds of color 2.
Do 3 rounds of color 1.
Do 5 rounds of color 5.
Taking only 1 turn around each arm do 1 round of color 6. Returning to pattern wrap, do 4 rounds of color 2.
Taking only 1 turn around each arm finish with 5 rounds of color 7.

FINISHING:
Cover an 8" green styrofoam circle, 2" thick, with flocked artificial evergreen sprays, available in floral supply houses. Set tree in center. Leave ends untrimmed, or attach double beads (See MAKING ENDS NEAT).

COLORS:
1. Variegated candy stripe
2. Emerald green
3. Mohair in green shades
4. Variegated green
5. Light green
6. Narrow gold braid
7. Dark green

FIESTA TIME IN JUAREZ

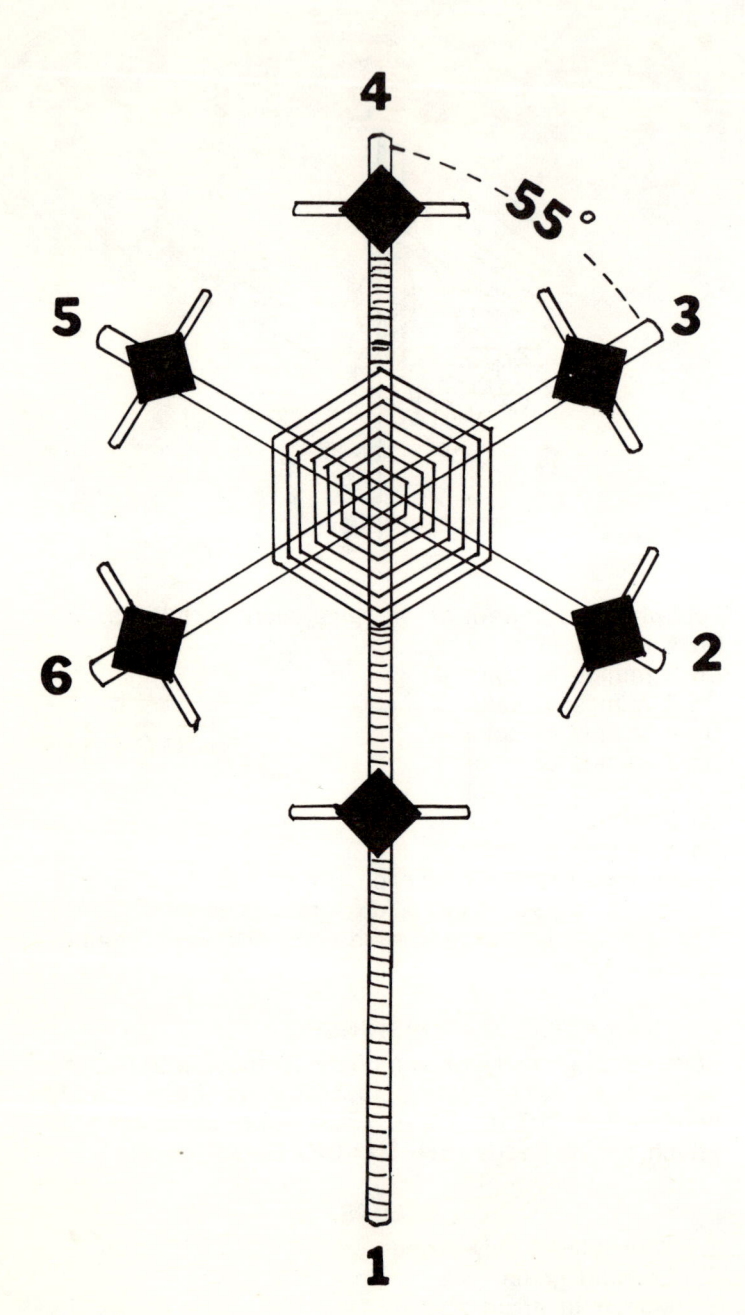

This simple delicate ojo is typical of the ones used in Mexican and Southwest Texas homes. Instead of being made in knitting wools on lumberyard sticks, it is constructed of the natural outdoor woods and single ply Persian yarns.

STICKS:

Select a tree limb that has a straight run of 16" to 18", and about ¼" in diameter. Cut two straight pieces the same diameter and 11" long. Cut 6 pieces 3" long and about ⅛" diameter.

NOTCHING:

Using your template, notch the two 11" sticks to fit at the 55° angle. Then notch back of long stick 6" down to fit on crossed sticks.

GLUING:

Glue to make angled shield as shown.

PROCEDURE:

With color 1, wrap each arm in succession, starting with arm 1, for 13 rounds, after crossing center 4 and 5 times to cover.

With color 2, do 7 rounds, wrapping each arm in succession.

With color 3, do 7 rounds, wrapping each arm in succession.

Now notch the BACK of arms 2, 3, 4, 5, 6, 1¼" down and deep enough to hold the 3" sticks; notching the long stick at the back 11" down, glue the 6 small sticks on as shown.

With color 4, wrapping each arm, do a half-inch eye. The eye will have a diamond appearance because of the different thickness of sticks.
With color 5, do 4 rounds.

With color 3, extend wrap exposed sticks on arms 2, 3, 5 and 6. Extend wrap arm 4 to meet ojo with a strand of colors 6 and 7 worked together. Also with same colors, extend wrap both above and below the lower small ojo on arm 1.

FINISHING:

Trim the two arms of the lower small ojo, and all 3 arms of each end small ojo with clown tassels (See MAKING ENDS NEAT) in color 6.

COLORS:

1. Lime green
2. Bright red
3. Teal blue
4. Royal blue
5. Bright orange
6. Bright green
7. Bright yellow

40

LAS FLECHAS DE SOL
(Arrows of the sun)

STICKS:
Cut four 24" and eight 6" sticks in narrow width.

NOTCHING:
Notch 24" sticks in center and also 3¼" in from each end. Notch 6" sticks in center. Bevel all ends.

GLUING:
Glue 6" sticks at 3¼" notches. Paint all sticks dark green.

PROCEDURE:
Work all four sticks alike, but do not join until they are all worked.

Attach color 1 on arm 1 and make a 1" half-eye (See TERMINOLOGY). With wall tree wrap (See TERMINOLOGY) do 4 rounds of color 2 taking 2 wraps on arm 3. Continuing tree wrap, do 4 rounds of color 3.

Attach color 4 on arm 2 with cut end toward bottom. Tree wrap arms 2, 1, 4 for 3 rounds. (About 1" of arm 1 will remain unwrapped).

With color 5 do 2 rounds in the same wrap.

With color 6 using tree wrap do 3 rounds.

FINISHING:
Glue sticks together to make two basic ojos. When glue is dry fasten ojos together in shield fashion by drilling a small hole through center. Secure with a brass screw and nut.

Glue Huicol sun god (See CENTER TRIMS) over center screw. Trim each arrow end with a cluster of three feathers, orange, yellow and green, tucked under wrapping.

COLORS:
1. Dark orange
2. Yellow Dazzleaire
3. Light orange
4. Light green
5. Light green Dazzleaire
6. Emerald green

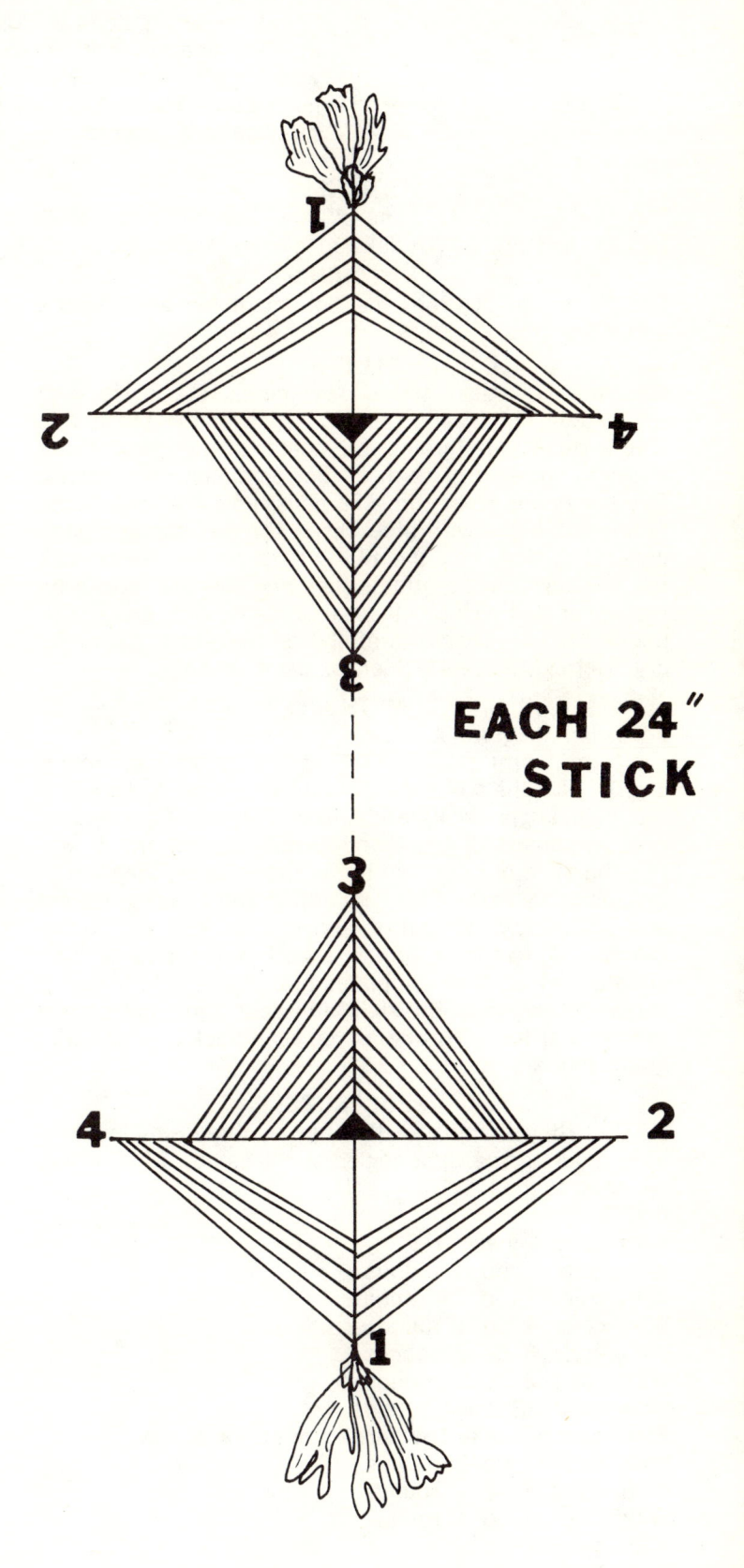

EACH 24" STICK

PARTY TIME

As shown, this ojo can be used as a centerpiece for Christmas or a golden wedding anniversary party. Made in white and silver it would be appropriate for a silver wedding anniversary. Made in all white, it could be used for a Confirmation. It may be trimmed with decorated satin balls if desired.

STICKS:
Cut one 36", one 17", one 8", and one 5½", two 8½", two 4", and two 2¾" sticks in narrow width.

NOTCHING:
On the 36" stick, from the bottom, notch at 11", 24", and 32½".

GLUING:
Glue the 17" stick at the lower notch, the 8" stick at the middle notch, and the 5½" stick at the top notch. Drill a small hole through the center of the glued sticks and into one end of each of the remaining short sticks. Cut the heads from three 2" nails, and file to a point. Filling the holes with glue, insert the nail through each crossed stick. Push the 8½" sticks on the lower nail, the 4" sticks on the middle nail, and the 2¾" sticks on the upper nail. This will make a right-angle cross with the 36" stick. Check carefully for the exact angle, let dry overnight, bevel all ends, paint white.

METHOD:
Following **Diagram A**, attach yarn back of arm 1, wind over arm 2, arm 3 and arm 4, ending by twirling around arm 1. Give the ojo a quarter turn to the right, disregard the right angle sticks and follow **Diagram B**, wrapping over arm 5, arm 3, arm 6 and twirling around arm 1. Rotate the ojo a quarter turn to the right. Follow **Diagram C**, wrapping over arm 4, arm 3, arm 2 and twirling around arm 1. Give ojo a quarter turn to the right and follow **Diagram D**, wrapping arm 6, arm 3, arm 5 and twirling around arm 1. This completes one round. (Hint: Clip a small clothespin to the right arm each time you start a new quarter turn. This helps you keep track of which Diagram you are on.)

PROCEDURE:
NOTE: (If you think of this ojo as three simple basic ojos, ignoring the right-angled sticks as you wind, it will be easy to do.)

OJO 1:
With color 1 make a 1" eye.
With color 2 do 3 rounds.
With color 3A do 3 rounds.
With color 4 do 1 round.
With color 5 do 2 rounds.
With color 2 do 3 rounds.
With color 3B do 4 rounds.
From now on, take two turns around each arm.
With color 1 do 2 rounds.
With color 5 do 2 rounds.
With color 6 do 1 round.
With color 7 do 3 rounds.
With color 8 do 3 rounds.
With color 1 do 1 round.
From now on, take two turns around arms 2, 4, 5 and 6.
With color 3B do 3 rounds.
With color 3A do 1 round.
Taking one turn around each arm, do 1 round of color 4.
Taking two turns around arms 2, 4, 5, 6 with color 8 do 2 rounds. With color 7 do 3 rounds.

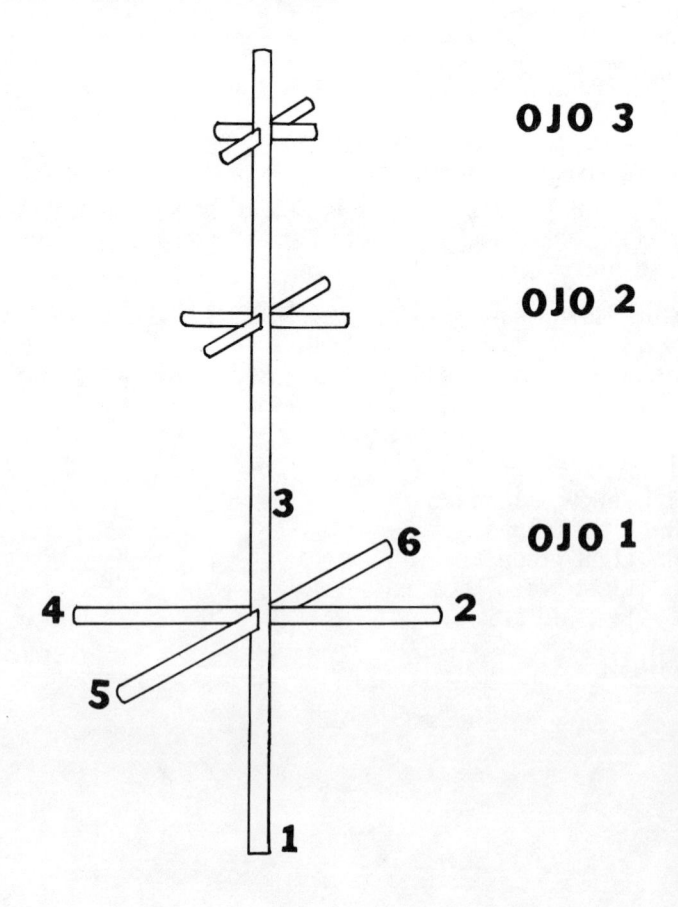

OJO 2:
With color 1 make a ½" eye.
With color 2 do 3 rounds.
With color 3A do 3 rounds.
With color 4 do 1 round.
With color 5 do 2 rounds.
With color 2 do 2 rounds.
With color 6 do 1 round.
With color 3B do 2 rounds.
With color 7 do 2 rounds.
With color 5 do 1 round.
With color 8 do 2 rounds.
With color 3A do 2 rounds.
With color 4 do 1 round.
With color 8 do 2 rounds.

PARTY TIME (Cont.)

OJO 3:
With color 1 make a ½" eye.
With color 2 do 2 rounds.
With color 3A do 1 round.
With color 4 do 1 round.
With color 5 do 1 round.
With color 3B do 2 rounds.
With color 6 do 1 round.
With color 7 do 2 rounds.

FINISHING:
Cut two pieces of white tulle, 6" wide and 24" long. Cut three pieces 6" wide and 12" long. (Available by the yard in fabric stores or in 6" wide rolls at a florist supply house.) Cut two of the 12" pieces in half lengthwise giving you four pieces 3" by 12". Lay two of the cut pieces along center of the wide piece (see diagram below), and using doubled sewing thread gather through the center. Tie each ruffle around the stick between ojos 1 and 2, and ojos 2 and 3. Run a gathering thread along each edge top and bottom and tie around center stick to make a pouff. String six gold glittered ½" white bells (available in card and florist shops) on doubled white thread and tie around center of pouff. Space evenly. Placing cut edges of last 6" by 12" piece together, to make a doubled 3" by 12" piece, run a gathering thread along cut edge. Tie snugly around end of arm 3 and trim with eight small bells.

Cut a 3", 4", and 6" round template from cardboard. Cut twelve pieces of tulle for each sized template. Laying three pieces together and running a line of glue around arm end, ¼" from arm end, place center of tulle circles over stick end and tie firmly with a 6" piece of color 4. Thread a small bell on each free end. Use the 6" circles on ojo 1, the 4" circles on ojo 2, and the 3" circles on ojo 3.

HANGING:
The ojo may be hung by inserting a small screw eye and a fishing swivel in the end of arm 3 or if it is to be used as a centerpiece, it may be inserted into a halved large white styrofoam ball. The base may be covered with metallic cloth. The ojo may also be set permanently into a Plexiglass base if desired.

COLORS:
1. White Wintuk
2. White Dawn Odyssey
3A. White Pliana separated to 1 ply
3B. White Pliana 2 ply
4. Round gold metallic cord
5. White bouclé
6. Flat gold metallic cord
7. White Wintuk Pompadour
8. White mohair

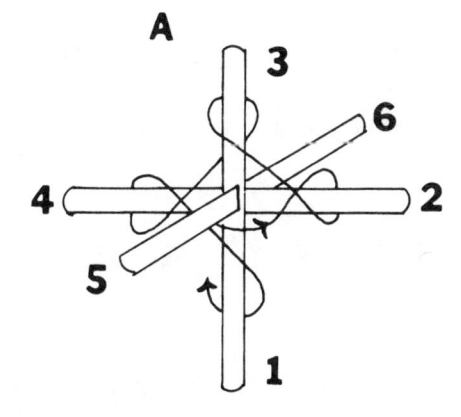

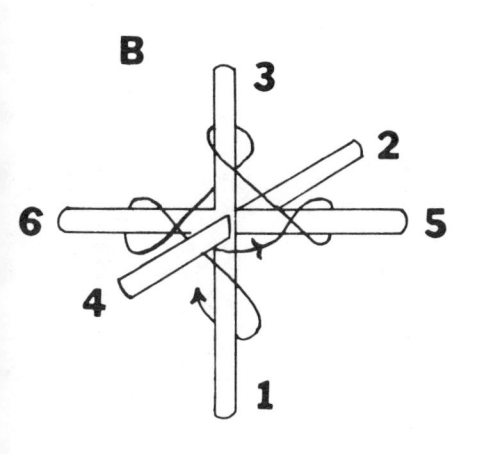

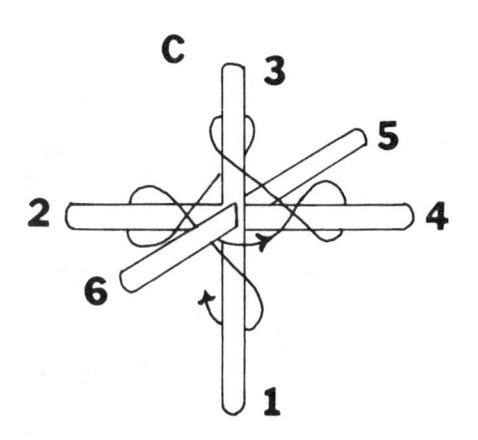

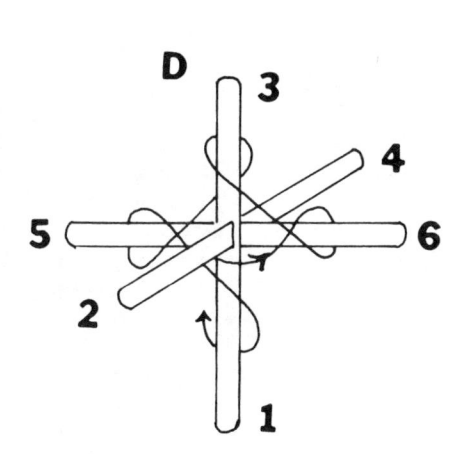

PLANTER POLE

By using a standard floor-to-ceiling planter pole, easily obtainable, it is possible to decorate a problem corner, or give the illusion of a small room divider with colorful ojos that act as mini-mobiles.

MATERIALS NEEDED:

You will need three 8" Box Wreath frames. These can be found in a florist supply store. Three fireplace matches will make the three mini-ojos. You will also need about three yards of DMC tapestry yarns, separated into single ply. The tear-drop jewels, seven of each color, may be found in craft stores.

PROCEDURE:

With wire cutters, trim off any excess ends on the Box Wreath frames. You may wrap these in wool, fancy yarns, or craft yarns. The ones pictured were wrapped in a textured yarn.

First, wrap all cross braces and glue off at top and bottom. Next, following wrapping diagram below, wrap over and around the outside wire, under and around the middle wire, under and around the inner wire. Carry thread under the middle wire and back over and around the outside wire with 2 turns, returning under and around the center wire. NOTE: If your yarn does not cover the projecting center wire completely, you may have to wind this wire first in the same way you did the cross braces.

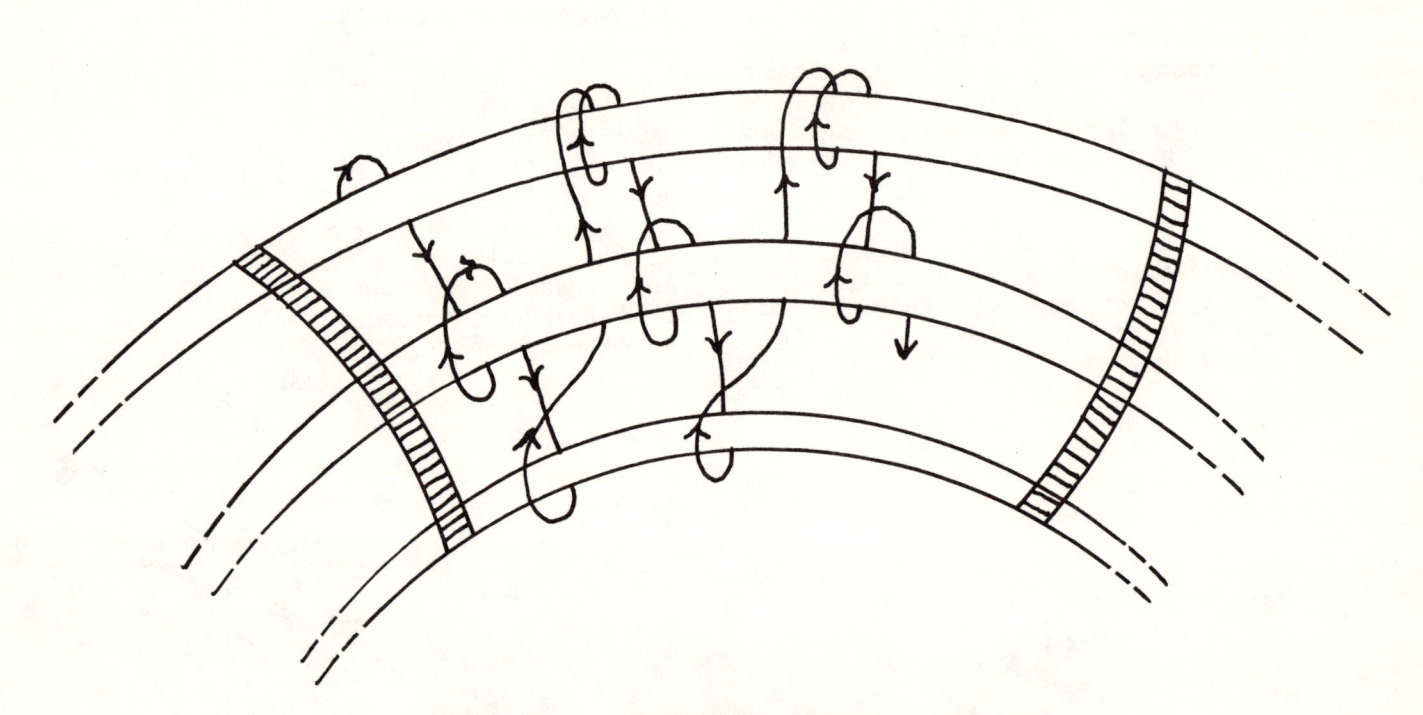

BOX WREATH RING

PLANTER POLE (Cont.)

Make three mini-ojos by cutting three fireplace matches into the following measurements: One 4" piece, two 2" pieces, and one 1⅞" piece. Following the diagram below, glue the 2" pieces ¾" from top and bottom of the 4" piece. Glue the short piece in the center of the 4" piece at right-angles to the other two arms.

Work all three mini-ojos alike using colors as given in chart below. With color 1 do a ¼" double eye at each cross. Extend wrap exposed stick between the eyes.

With color 2, following method below, do 2 rounds. With color 3 do 2 rounds. With color 4, do 1 round. With color 5, do 2 rounds.

METHOD:

Glue color 2 behind arm 1 and bring to front. Holding firmly by arm 8, go over and around arm 2, cross the center stick and go over and around arm 7. Recross the center stick and go over and around arm 3, over and around arm 4, over and around arm 5, over and around arm 7, over and around arm 6, over and around arm 1 with a half turn.

Now holding ojo by arm 7, repeat the pattern by going over and around arm 6, cross the center stick, going over and around arm 8, recross the center stick going over and around arm 5, over and around arm 4, over and around arm 3, over and around arm 8, over and around arm 2, over and around arm 1 with a half turn.
Holding by arm 8, repeat the diagrams A and B for a complete pattern.

Continue wrapping in this fashion, changing colors on arm 1 as desired. BE SURE YOU HAVE COMPLETED **DIAGRAM B** BEFORE CHANGING COLOR.

TRIMMING:

With a piece of matching thread, tie a small tear-drop jewel to arms 1, 2, 4, 5, 6, 7, 8, reinforcing with a dab of glue. Using nylon thread, attach a small fishing swivel to arm 3. Insert a jump ring in top loop of swivel and clamp around cross brace at center wire. With two links of anodized drapery chain, clamp at top bar of cross brace for hanging.

COLORS:

OJO 1. (Frame wrapped in Unger #9 in shades of rose, peach, purple)
1. Raspberry DMC #7600
2. Peach DMC #7852
3. Dark blue DMC #7797
4. Fine white boucle'
5. Coral DMC #7851

OJO 2. (Frame wrapped in Unger #9 in shades of green/blue/yellow)
1. Emerald DMC #7943
2. Light blue DMC #7599
3. Medium green DMC #7912
4. Fine white boucle'
5. Medium blue DMC #7798

OJO 3. (Frame wrapped in Unger #9 in shades of gold/yellow/cream)
1. Dark orange DMC #7439
2. Gold DMC #7742
3. Brown DMC #7444
4. Fine white boucle'
5. Apricot DMC #7437

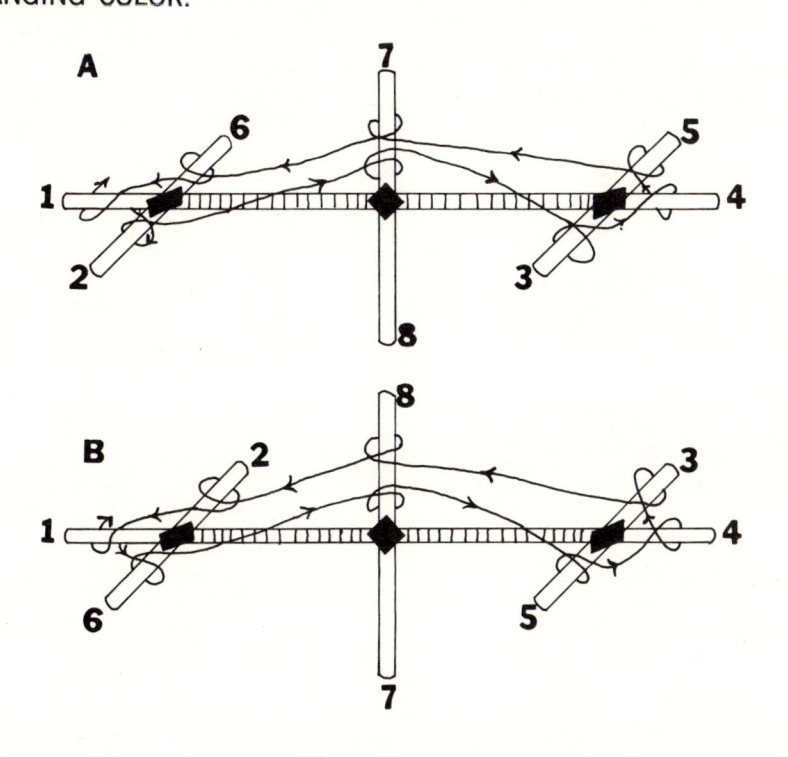

AMERICAN SPACE SHUTTLE

An all-American red, white and blue beauty, this ojo would be equally attractive in any combination of colors.

STICKS:
Cut one 24", one 16" and two 8" sticks in narrow width.

NOTCHING:
Notch the 24" stick 8" down from top and 16" stick in center.

GLUING:
Glue the two notched sticks together to form a kite shape. Cut the head from a 2" nail and file to point. Drill a small hole through the center of the glued notches and into one end of each of the 8" sticks. Fill each hole with glue, insert nail through notch hole and into each 8" stick to make a right angle cross with kite shape. Check carefully to see each stick is square with the adjoining stick. Let dry overnight. Paint bright blue.

METHOD:
Following **Diagram A,** attach yarn back of arm 1, wind over arm 2, arm 3 and arm 4, ending by twirling around arm 1. Give the ojo a quarter turn to the right, disregard the right angle sticks and follow **Diagram B,** wrapping over arm 5, arm 3, arm 6 and twirling around arm 1. Rotate the ojo a quarter turn to the right. Follow **Diagram C,** wrapping over arm 4, arm 3 arm 2 and twirling around arm 1. Give ojo a quarter turn to the right and follow **Diagram D,** wrapping arm 6, arm 3, arm 5 and twirling around arm 1. This completes one round. (Hint: Clip a small clothespin to the right arm each time you start a new quarter turn. This helps you keep track of which Diagram you are on.)

Note: If you think of this ojo as a simple kite ojo, ignoring the right angle sticks as you wind, it will be easy to do.

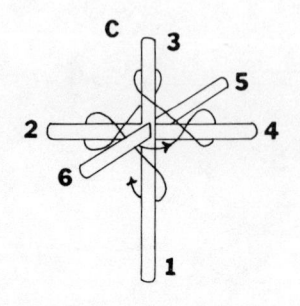

PROCEDURE:
With color 1, wrap an eye of 5 rounds.
Attach color 2 behind arm 1 (always glue off and glue new color on behind arm 1) and start Kite Wrap with two turns on arm 1 and one turn on all other arms. Do 4 complete rounds.
Attach color 3 and do 2 complete rounds.
Attach color 1 and do 2 complete rounds.
Attach color 4 and do 4 complete rounds.
Attach color 2 and do 2 complete rounds.
Attach color 1 and do 4 complete rounds.
Attach color 3 and do 3 complete rounds.
Attach color 4 and do 4 complete rounds.
Attach color 2 and finish with 2 complete rounds.

Now, turn ojo upside down and hold by arm 3.

TAKING TWO TURNS AROUND EACH ARM:
Attach color 3 to arm 2 on what is now the underside of arm 2.
Top wrap arms 2, 6, 4 and 5 in succession for 3 rounds.
With color 1, do 3 rounds.
With color 4, do 6 rounds.
With color 2, do 2 rounds.

Trim arms 2, 6, 4 and 5 with small size satellite pompons (See MAKING ENDS NEAT).

Attach a small fishing swivel on arm 1 by using a screw eye.

Attach a jump ring and hang by arm 1.

COLOR CHART
1. Bucilla Frisky in pink/red/white combination
2. Royal blue
3. White
4. Bright red

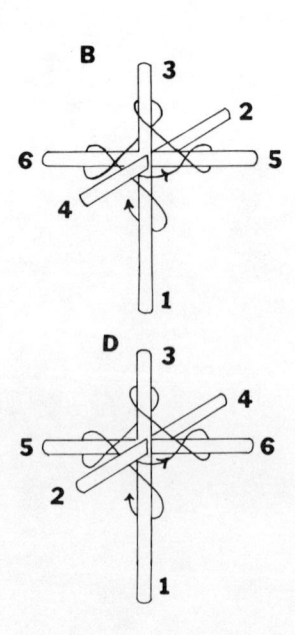

FIJI FAN

While on a recent trip to the South Pacific, the author attended a ceremonial Meke given by a Fijian Ethnic Dance Group. One of the dance numbers represented the warriors of the 1800's. Performed solely by men, the dancers held sharpened spears in their right hand and carried in their left hands a protective fan made of reinforced coconut palm fronds and trimmed on one side with an ojo wound in wool. These fans are not made for sale as they have a religious significance. In war against an enemy, the fan was turned toward the antagonist to invoke protection of the gods and asking that the spears go straight to the mark.

On learning of the Creative Ojo Books, one of the dancers formally presented the author with the fan pictured in this book. It is so unusual, directions for reproducing it are included here.

If you live in an area where palm fronds are available, you may make your own fan base, shaped as shown in the diagram below. If you do not have access to the fronds, you may purchase a fan as nearly the right size as possible, trimming to size, or adjusting the wire teardrops to fit your purchased fan.

MATERIALS:

You will need 60 pieces of 30 gauge florist wire, 28" long, and 60 pieces 22½" long. You will also need a wide stick 8½" long, or you may use a piece of ½" dowel, for the handle of the fan. You will also need some extra pieces of palm frond for trimming, or you may use corn husk, obtainable in craft shops. For the ojo, you will need two bar-b-q sticks, one 8" long and one 6" long.

PROCEDURE:

If you are making your own fan, start by making a center reinforcing frame of a 12" piece of narrow width stick, secured firmly to the last inch of your handle stick. Lay this reinforcing stick between two pieces of palm frond and fasten with buttonhole twist at three points. Trim frond to shape shown in diagram below.

If you are using a ready made fan, trim to fit shape in diagram. From now on both a palm frond or a bought fan will be worked the same way.

Cut pieces of palm frond (or corn husk) 2½" long, making the ends jagged. Overlapping as necessary, glue these pieces, facing outward, around both back and front of the fan's outer edge.

(When working with corn husks, they must be damp. See CORN HUSK OWL p. 37.)

Divide wires into bunches of 30 pieces. Fasten together with tape at both ends. Shape as shown in diagram. Wind each bundle closely with wool in varying colors. Placing one small and one large wire teardrop on each side of fan, trim so each teardrop fits within the next one. Fasten securely by stitching through the saw-tooth trimming.

Attach a frond 18" long to handle at base of wires. Use two 4" pieces at top tucking between saw-tooth trim. Wind handle completely with wool.

Gluing bar-b-q sticks together at centers, wind a simple 3½" basic ojo using colors as desired. Slip bar-b-q sticks under the front wires, gluing in place if necessary. Place a hanging loop on the back wire.

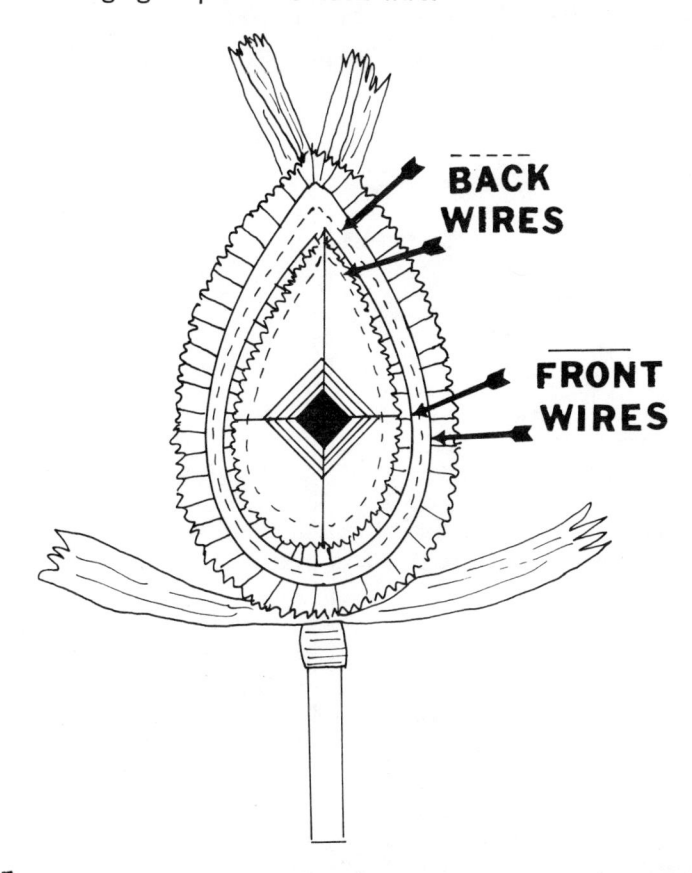

TITANIA

The breathtaking sparkle of this ojo makes it a decoration fit for Titania, Shakespeare's Queen of Fairyland.

STICKS:
Cut one 36", one 24", two 12", four 8", two 6", and twelve 3" sticks all in narrow width.

NOTCHING:
Notch the 36" and the 24" sticks in the center. Notch the 36" stick 4" in from each end. Notch the 24" stick 3" in from each end. Notch the two 12" sticks 3" in from one end. Notch the 8" and 6" sticks in the center. Bevel the ends of the 12" sticks closest to the notches. Leave other ends unbeveled. Bevel one end of the 3" sticks. Bevel both ends of the 36", 24", 8", and 6" sticks.

GLUING:
Glue the 24" and 36" sticks together at the center notch. Cut head from 2" nail and file to point. Drill small hole through center of glued sticks and into one end of each 12" stick. Fill hole with glue and insert nail through basic ojo cross. Fill 12" stick holes with glue and push onto nail to make a right angle cross with basic cross. Check carefully for exact angle. Let dry overnight.
Note: The main ojo is completely worked before gluing on the end sticks. Paint all sticks magenta red.

PROCEDURE:
Note: If you think of this ojo as a simple basic ojo, ignoring the right angle sticks as you wind, it will be easy to do.

METHOD:
Following **Diagram A**, attach yarn back of arm 1, wind over arm 2, arm 3 and arm 4, ending by twirling around arm 1. Give the ojo a quarter turn to the right, disregard the right angle sticks and follow **Diagram B**, wrapping over arm 5, arm 3, arm 6 and twirling around arm 1. Rotate the ojo a quarter turn to the right. Follow **Diagram C**, wrapping over arm 4, arm 3, arm 2 and twirling around arm 1. Give ojo a quarter turn to the right and follow **Diagram D**, wrapping arm 6, arm 3, arm 5 and twirling around arm 1. This completes one round. (Hint: Clip a small clothespin to the right arm each time you start a new quarter turn. This helps you keep track of which Diagram you are on.)

With color 1 do 1¾" eye.
With color 2 do 5 rounds.

With color 3 do 1 round. Be sure to stretch elastic yarn evenly.

With color 4 do 5 rounds.
With color 5 do 4 rounds.
With color 1 do 2 rounds.
With color 3 do 1 round.
With color 2 do 4 rounds.
With color 5 do 2 rounds.
With color 4 do 4 rounds.
With color 1 do 5 rounds.
With color 3 do 1 round.
With color 5 do 3 rounds.
With color 2 do 4 rounds.
With color 1 do 5 rounds.
With color 4 do 3 rounds.
With color 3 do 1 round.

TITANIA (Cont.)

End Ojos

Glue 8" sticks on arms 2, 4, 5, and 6. Glue 6" sticks on arms 1 and 3. Using same method of nailing through center, attach 3" sticks at right angles to each end ojo.

Working exactly the same method as for the big ojo, make matching end ojos as follows:

Mark arm 1 of each end ojo with a small piece of masking tape and work each ojo in a vertical plane so arm 1 is pointing toward floor as the ojo hangs. Before winding, attach a small fishing swivel by inserting a screw eye in top of arm 3 on big ojo, and connecting with a jump ring. The ojo should be wound while hanging.

With color 1 do 6 rounds.
With color 2 do 5 rounds.
With color 3 do 1 round.
With color 4 do 4 rounds.
With color 5 do 3 rounds.
With color 1 do 3 rounds.
With color 3 do 1 round.

FINISHING:

Cluster six small magenta colored stemmed glass balls, such as used in holiday decorations around arms 1 and 3 at the end of the big ojo.

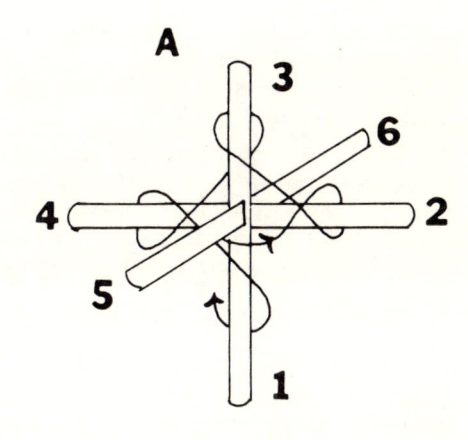

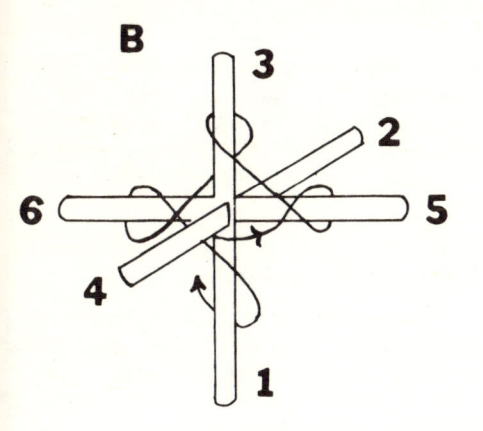

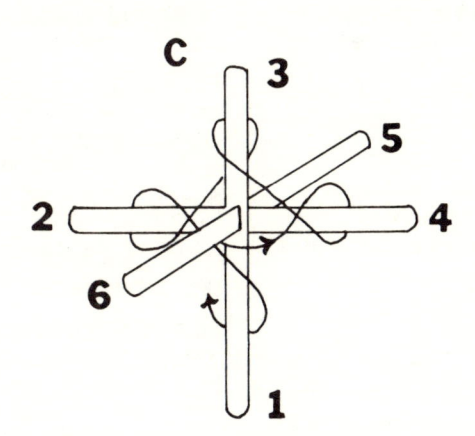

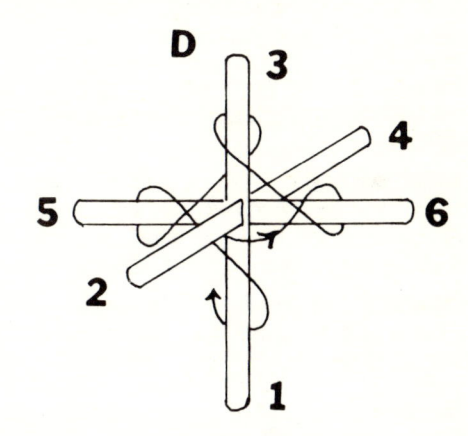

COLORS:

1. Magenta Persian. Separate into 1 and 2 strand balls. Always wrap with 2 strand. You will need three 40 yard skeins.
2. Pink Madison bouclé from Israel. You will need one skein.
3. Magenta Tinsel Stretch Gift Tie. You will need four 15 foot cards.
4. White and silver Soireé.
5. Rose pink bouclé.

COLOR CHOICES

Traditional ojos are made in earth colors in Indian country — browns, reds, whites, grays, oranges, greens. The eye is usually made dark. Ojos from other parts of the world are not so stylized and the eye may be any color desired. Colors used in the ojo are limited only by your imagination or colors in use in the room where your ojo will hang.

While some mono-tone ojos are unusually beautiful — such as one using several shades of orange, or a blend of greens — most ojos are more attractive with the use of at least 2 different colors in at least 3 shades. If you are uncertain what colors will look good on your ojo, make a mini ojo first using a strand or two of each color. It can be used as a package tie when you are done, and you will have the effect of the colors you have chosen.

The colors you paint your sticks may be the same shade as the outside wind of yarn, or they may be in direct contrast to the yarn you finish winding with, picking up one of your inside colors. Highly sophisticated ojos are sometimes made on gilded or silvered sticks, wound of nylon yarns in striking colors. The ojo can be as modern or as traditional as you wish.

The use of different textures of yarns in one ojo makes for interest and artistic effect. Be careful when you use specialty yarns that your tension will hold. If the yarn has no stretch, it will be necessary to anchor it with glue on each arm to keep it from sagging.

YARN SUBSTITUTES

When no other specification is given in the color chart or the ojo directions, the yarn used is 4 ply knitting yarn. It may be either wool or mixtures, it makes no difference in the amount of windings used. When yarns are to be divided into separate ply counts — such as Persian yarns — the directions specify.

Many times the yarns are either not available except in larger stores or certain areas of the country. In this case, you may have to substitute yarns in the directions. The following guide should be helpful:

MADISON is a single ply yarn from Israel. It has a bumpy boucle appearance, is a cotton yarn and any single or lightweight two-ply yarn may be used instead.

SOIREÉ is a yarn from France. It is a two ply, one ply of wool yarn, the second ply a metallic thread. To get the same effect, you may use a baby yarn or 2-ply Persian and work a metallic thread along with it. The two should be twisted together and wound together before using.

PLIANA is an acrylic yarn similar to a craft yarn of medium weight, 3 ply.

DAZZLEAIRE is a mohair-type knitting worsted. A regular mohair may be substituted.

REYNOLD'S VENDOME can be interchanged with any sport yarn.

MAKING ENDS NEAT
(Continued from page 8)

DOUBLE BEAD ENDS: Cut a 9" piece of wool to match a 1" diameter wood bead. Loop yarn and push loop up through bead center. Fasten over end of arm, tacking with glue if necessary. String a smaller bead (large enough not to go through big bead hole) on cut ends and knot tightly against larger bead with simple finger knot.

ARROWHEADS: These effective trims are available at most stores carrying Indian items or souvenir items. Glued to stick ends, or even on eye, they give a true Indian appearance to your ojo.

FRENCH TASSELS: While the regular cardboard wound tassel can be used, the French tassel is far more attractive and is easily made. Wind the regular tassel on a piece of cardboard, allowing 1½ inches more than the desired length, (e.g. if you want a tassel which measures 6", cut the cardboard 7½" long). Tie at the top in the usual fashion, and tie around top as though making a simple tassel. Then flip tassel upside down, holding by tied part. Tie again, this time below the first tie. Carefully pull up two strands of yarn from opposite sides for attaching to ojo.

SHOOTING TASSELS: Start by making a regular French tassel around cardboard pattern and tying the threads together at the top. Then dipping end of ojo arm ¼" into glue, arrange tassel pieces around stick end pointing **TOWARD** the eye of the ojo. Tie firmly just above glue line. Let dry thoroughly. Then bring ends back toward end of stick and tie firmly just below the stick end. (Shooting tassels should be short enough to stand out and not droop.)

FEATHERS: One of the more traditional trims for ojos is the use of feathers. They can be used singly or in groups at the ends of the sticks. To apply, wrap stick with same wool as last top or back wrap, glue feathers about ½ inch back on sticks, and rewrap with same wool to cover feather spine.

PRAYER STICK FEATHERS: These are described in detail under **Navaho Brave** and **Party Time.**

FEATHER TASSELS: Another use of feathers is to make feather tassels. Attach a cluster of 4 or 5 small feathers to a piece of leather thong by knotting into end. With wool, wrap top of feathers covering knot. String several colored wooden beads on thong. With wool, cover balance of thong and leave end for tying to ojo arm.

COCKADED TASSEL: A different version of the shooting tassel is made by cutting the tassel pieces an extra ½" in length, tying as directed for shooting tassel, then combing with a wire pet brush, or similar stiff bristled brush while lying on a flat surface. Be careful not to pull out too much of the yarn fibre. Then while still lying flat, trim into an arc shape with the center left the highest point. NOTE: Some yarns will not brush out; try a few pieces before making tassel.

MAKING A TEMPLATE

To make anything other than a regular right-angle cross ojo frame, it is necessary to calculate angles very carefully. To do this, make a good template which can be used for all special ojos.

Using a piece of poster board or a letter-sized sheet of paper, draw a perfect circle. You may use a plate, pot lid or a compass. Find the center and mark with a small circle dot. Draw the vertical and horizontal lines which bisect the circle. These will be your guide lines for either vertical or horizontal base sticks, whenever called for

With a protractor on the vertical line, mark for 30°, 45° and 60° angles. These are the ones you will usually use. Draw them in on the circle. If you wish, you may use different colored lines for each angle.

When notching angled sticks, always be sure to mark the center and place the mark on your template center.

One caution, if you are making a 3-stick angled frame, where the vertical stick is not marked in the center, but at a stated measurement up or down from the end, then place that marking, such as 5" up from bottom, on the center of the template when laying the crossed sticks on top for notching.

When placing the sticks, be sure to place the center of the stick on the line, not the edge of the stick. And when there is no vertical stick used, be careful to figure it as the angle cross. For example, when the directions say place the two sticks at 30° angle to the vertical, this means the sticks are laid on the 30° line even though no vertical stick will be used. Always notch and glue the angle sticks, then place on the vertical or horizontal stick and notch only the lower stick for the final gluing.

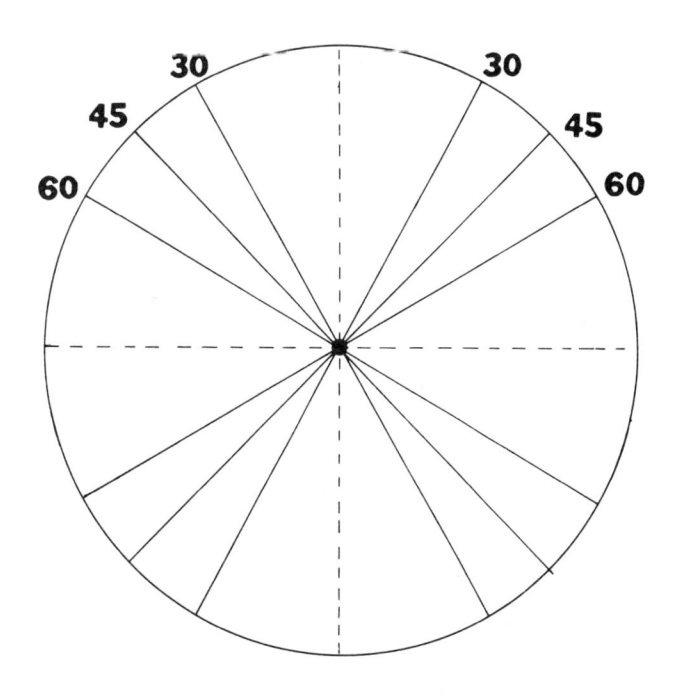

HELPFUL HINTS

In the first two books of this series, many hints were given as to selecting color schemes, attaching feathers, protecting your ojo when shipping, or from dirt accumulation. These additional hints should help you in ojo construction.

TWIRLING: Yarn may be wound by the "throw" or "twirling" method. Twirling is more desirable. Instead of looping the yarn around each arm, hold each arm in succession in left hand, yarn in right, spin ojo completely around letting yarn wind around arm required number of turns. Keeping yarn in right hand, turn ojo ¼ turn to right, change hand from previous arm to new arm and repeat spin.

COUNTERWEIGHTS: When you make an ojo and attach an unevenly balanced trim to the main ojo (such as in Barn Owl), you will have to use counterweights to keep the ojo hanging evenly. Lead counterweights are available at small cost at any hobby shop carrying model railroad items. They have a self-adhesive backing and you will attach them on the arm opposite to the arm which tends to swing downward. Stick to the back side or hide inside wrapping.

When working on small ojos made with small sticks, use #0 metal clips to hold yarn after gluing. These are available in drug and variety stores, or office supply houses.

On extremely long wraps, toward the outside edge of a basic ojo, or on wing wraps extending some distance across sticks, your thread may tend to bunch. To keep threads flat, take an extra wind around each arm. You may always use an extra wind without destroying the pattern of an ojo whenever the yarn is not lying flat.

Whenever you work within circles such as embroidery hoops, or within such special shapes as Box Wreath rings, wind your yarn into small balls. Try to estimate how much you will need to complete your pattern, then add a few extra inches for any extra arm winds you may have to make. If the small balls will not pass through the enclosed wrapping space, "butterfly" your yarn as for macrame work.

If your glue tends to thicken too much while using it, cut a small circle of cardboard the size of your bottle opening, punch a hole through the center and insert a barbeque stick. You may then use the stick as an applicator and the cardboard will keep the air from your glue.

If you must thin glue, do it by adding water with an eyedropper to avoid thinning too much.

If you are working an ojo design that is either too heavy or too large to handle easily by twirling, fix a temporary swivel hook at top (See TITANIA) and wind while suspended from a hook or a chain.

If you make a nursery ojo mobile and wish to keep it out of the reach of a small child, staple a nylon thread to your ceiling and fasten the ojo to the thread. It will seem suspended in air, will not mar your ceiling and will eliminate any danger of children pulling it down.